CROSVILLE IN LIVERPOOL

RICHARD LLOYD JONES

This book is dedicated to the staff that worked for Crosville in Liverpool over its sixty-five-year presence in the city and to their families.
It is also dedicated to my family who have listened to me patiently as I have put this book together, often typing into the night. My family's support in the continued preservation of former Crosville Bristol RELH6G, fleet number CRG163, has been invaluable.
I also dedicate this book to my dear father who sadly passed away from a short illness in March 2025, before he could see the book published. His support with the book and CRG163 was incredible.

Front cover, above: On 24 August 1986, two months from deregulation day, DVG274 is seen at Love Lane depot in its traditional NBC green, whilst DVL443 on the right has adopted the company's new post-deregulation identity of marigold orange and brunswick green. (Robert J. Montgomery); *below*: ERL310 at Mann Island, Pier Head, Liverpool, on the Saturday X10 service from Cemaes Bay, Anglesey, on 4 October 1984. (Robert J. Montgomery)
Back cover: DVG274 is seen here at the back of the yard at Love Lane, Liverpool, on 24 August 1986. Behind the barrier is the Leeds–Liverpool canal. When the allocation moved to this location, DVG 270/1/3/4/5 were the five of the HTU-N batch here, all being easy and pleasant to drive, as Robert Montgomery remembers. DVG274 was his personal favourite. (Robert J. Montgomery)

First published 2025

Amberley Publishing
The Hill, Stroud,
Gloucestershire, GL5 4EP

www.amberley-books.com

Copyright © Richard Lloyd Jones, 2025

The right of Richard Lloyd Jones to be identified as the Author
of this work has been asserted in accordance with the
Copyright, Designs and Patents Act 1988.

All rights reserved. No part of this book may be reprinted
or reproduced or utilised in any form or by any electronic,
mechanical or other means, now known or hereafter invented,
including photocopying and recording, or in any information
storage or retrieval system, without the permission in writing
from the Publishers.

ISBN: 978 1 3981 2262 8 (print)
ISBN: 978 1 3981 2263 5 (ebook)

British Library Cataloguing in Publication Data.
A catalogue record for this book is available from the British Library.

Typeset in 10pt on 13pt Celeste.
Origination by Amberley Publishing.
Printed in the UK.

Appointed GPSR EU Representative: Easy Access System Europe Oü, 16879218
Address: Mustamäe tee 50, 10621, Tallinn, Estonia
Contact Details: gpsr.requests@easproject.com, +358 40 500 3575

Contents

	Acknowledgements	5
1	Crosville Connection	7
2	Crosville	10
3	Edge Lane Depot	14
	Transport Act 1947	16
	Transport Act 1968	19
	Merseyside Passenger Transport Executive	21
	The National Bus Company	23
	Professional and Proud	27
	Trade Union/Management Relationship	32
	Fleet Size	36
	Market Analysis Project	38
	Transport Act 1980	40
4	Crosville Liverpool in Photographs	42
5	Edge Lane Depot Closure	51
6	Love Lane Depot	55
	The Transport Act 1985	56
	Preparing for Deregulation	58
	MCW Metroliner Coaches for National Express	64
	Deregulation, Major Contract Wins and Closure	66
7	The Silent Depot	79
8	Personal Recollection of Paul Rycroft	81
9	Mr Robert Parry MP	86
10	Crosville Beyond Love Lane	88
	Conclusion	93

A wonderful monochrome image of some of Crosville's Edge Lane depot staff in January 1980. They were regulars on the Liverpool/North Wales duties and are seen here standing in front of a CRG class coach at Edge Lane in the final week before the express work passed to National Travel. From left to right: driver Jimmy Timpson, conductor Les Coates, driver Bob Hayden, conductor Jack Jones and driver Ken Davies. (Bill Barlow)

Garage drivers Jimmy Allum and Frank Roddan in front of CRG163 at Edge Lane depot, 1978/1979. Frank was also the driver instructor at the depot for many years. John Embleton remembers arriving back at Edge Lane after just passing his PSV test at Chester. Jimmy and Frank were standing outside the canteen. 'Did you pass? Yes! Right into the coach park, lesson 1 how to manoeuvre coaches in a tight space.' 'The lessons carried on from then from two great people I will never forget.' (Bill Barlow)

Acknowledgements

A number of people have made valued contributions in the production of this book. A special thank you to Bill Barlow, Andrew Cudbertson, John Embleton, David Forrest, David A. Jones, Mike Lambden, Gethin Lloyd-Jones, Ioan Lloyd-Jones, Robert J. Montgomery, Geoff O'Brien, Raymond Patterson, Paul Rycroft, Les A. Smith, Robert Smith and Graham Warren.

Preserved CRG163 at Woodside, Birkenhead, in October 2005. The image recreates a daily occurrence back in the day when these elegant coaches operated long-distance services from Liverpool. (Richard Lloyd Jones)

Also much appreciated are documents and photographs supplied by The Bus Archive, Fred Burnett, Dave Cousins, Bob Downham, Brian Moore, John Lee and Geoff Smith.

Precious memories, some emotional, as well as documents and photographs of Crosville in Liverpool have been provided that have not been publicly seen before. Images bring the story alive and convey far more than just words on a page. The images within this book have certainly done that.

Graham Warren represents his dad George Warren, one of the 'legends' of Liverpool depot, who sadly passed away in 2016. We remember your dear dad, who would be extremely proud of you for telling his story.

I feel extremely privileged and honoured to have been a part of this important journey with the people named above in telling the story of what happened back then. It has been pieced together with the utmost care and respect to all concerned at all times. My ambition throughout has been to show the human aspect and the profound impact the closure of Crosville in Liverpool had on those concerned and their families.

I hope that this book does justice in the way it documents Crosville's proud history in Liverpool and then the events that led to the closure of its Love Lane depot.

We are all now the custodians of Crosville in ensuring that the name is kept alive out of respect for those who worked for the company and not just consigned to history. Nowadays there are generations that never knew that such a name existed and are now being told the story.

In memory with the greatest of respect.

Richard Lloyd Jones FCILT FCMI CMgr FIOM

1

Crosville Connection

My maternal grandfather worked as a conductor for Crosville Motor Services, or 'Crosville' as known by all, at its Blaenau Ffestiniog depot following his time as a soldier in the Second World War. Other relations, Arwyn and Huw Williams, also worked as clerks from the same depot. My paternal grandfather's brother, Idris Lloyd Jones, was a driver at Crosville's Flint depot.

I grew up with Crosville as a passenger, before school work experience with Crosville Wales in 1987 at its newly established HQ at Llandudno Junction depot. I also worked for the company during school holidays at its various offices before becoming full-time at

My grandfather Owen Islwyn Davies can be seen in the back row, far left. (Crosville Motor Services)

its Caernarfon depot, which sadly closed its doors through a company restructure at the beginning of 1991. I then trained as a bus driver at the young age of eighteen.

The bus industry was quite volatile at that time, as bus tenders were won and lost. I therefore ended up driving at many of the company's depots and outstations before moving to other roles in the bus industry.

Since 2002, I have also owned a former Crosville coach for restoration and preservation. The vehicle was originally based at Crosville's Edge Lane depot from new in 1970, operating the prestigious London-Liverpool coach service.

In researching the vehicle's history spanning fifty plus years, it has led me to Liverpool.

Growing up amongst green Crosville buses I have fond memories of many journeys by bus. Local staff were more than helpful with my persistent questioning about all things Crosville, which only spurred on my interest further. My grateful thanks to each and every one.

My paternal grandmother was born in Toxteth, Liverpool, on 7 April 1919 as my great-grandfather had moved from Blaenau Ffestiniog to Liverpool as a young adult in the early 1900s to work at the famous Cammell Laird ship builders in Birkenhead.

Me as a young twenty-one-year-old driver in front of Crosville Cymru/Wales STL47 at Porthmadog in 1993. (Richard Lloyd Jones)

Whilst in Liverpool he met my great-grandmother, who had also moved from the same part of Wales to the city. They both married and had a daughter, Lilly, my grandmother. Later on the family returned to Wales, to my great-grandfather's native town of Blaenau Ffestiniog.

Having read years ago about the sad end of Crosville in Liverpool, I have been keen since then to find out what exactly happened nearly forty years ago. I would have been fourteen years old at the time of the closure and living in North West Wales without a car meant I had very little knowledge of Crosville in Liverpool then. I always knew that one day I would be compelled to research what happened out of a sense of responsibility to tell the complete story on behalf of the people involved and their families.

This book started off as an online article following years of research, respectfully written and added to my preserved vehicle's website and shared on the Crosville Facebook groups. It was positively received, with encouragement to produce it in book form. Since then, the book has become far, far more than the original article. It has involved countless hours of further research, telephone calls, email exchanges, online meetings and other means to share and capture information for inclusion in the book. This culminated in a gathering (and reunion for many past company employees) at Crosville's former Edge Lane site in Liverpool to meet those who were actually involved at the time and their families.

Of everything I've ever written to date, this has got to be the most important, due to the gravity of the subject matter. Hopefully I've been able to factually document what led to the closure, but more importantly place the feelings and emotions of real people front and centre of the story.

2

Crosville

On 27 October 1906 the Crosville Motor Company was formed by George Crosland Taylor and his French business associate George de Ville. Its purpose initially was to assemble and sell French-designed cars and marine engines with company premises at Crane Wharf, Chester. The name Crosville was formed from an amalgamation of the names of both

The fifth and last Crosville car. (Crosville Motor Services)

founders, that being *Cros*land and *Ville*s. George Crosland Taylor, or Crosland as he was known, was the son of mill owner Henry Dyson Taylor and his wife Sarah. Car-making activities ceased in 1908, with the company instead focussing its activities on agency work and repairs.

George Crosland Taylor's son Edward, appointed company general manager in June 1908, purchased a Herald charabanc at auction in Swansea. Crosville approached Chester City Council in December 1910 requesting permission to start a new bus service, which was subsequently granted.

On 2 February 1911 the company started its first bus service between Chester and Ellesmere Port, having been advised to diversify its business into passenger transport. Once established, it was later extended to New Ferry, and a second new bus service was introduced between Chester and Kelsall.

Crosville then began to expand its operations into mid-Cheshire, predominantly around Crewe in December 1913 when the council approved licences for services in the area. This included acquiring the established business of Ward Brothers. The company's fleet livery at this time was grey.

DAILY MOTOR BUS SERVICE BETWEEN CHESTER, WHITBY AND ELLESMERE PORT.

TIME TABLES AND FARES UNTIL FURTHER NOTICE.

Crosville's bus timetable between Chester and Ellesmere Port, 20 June 1914. (Crosville Motor Co. Ltd)

Wartime restricted further expansion until 1919. Crosville introduced a Chester circular service along with other destinations established from Chester, as well as a New Ferry to Meols route.

In February 1929 company ownership changed when the London, Midland & Scottish Railways Company (LMS) purchased the Crosville Motor Company Limited due its losing passengers to road traffic. The company was purchased outright for £398,750. The Crosville Motor Company was placed into voluntary liquidation in November 1929. A new company trading as LMS (Crosville) was then introduced. Claude Crosland Taylor, who was the son of the original company founder, became the manager of the new business. The fleet livery at this time was maroon.

In 1930 the company changed again arising from an agreement made between the railway companies and the Tilling and British Automobile Traction Group (T&BAT) to acquire 50 per cent of the shareholdings of each company under the group's control. In return the railway companies sold 50 per cent of their shareholdings in acquired businesses to the T&BAT. In some cases new companies were formed; however, in relation to LMS (Crosville), Crosville Motor Services Ltd emerged on 15 May 1930, with LMS having only owned Crosville outright for nine months. Claude Crosland Taylor was retained as the new company's general manager, maintaining the family/company connection.

As new depots were built by the company so too were new friendships and communities, the company affectionately becoming known as the Crosville family. Staff who worked for the company were extremely proud to do so.

George Crosland Taylor, company founder and chairman 1906–23. (Crosville Motor Services)

Expansion of the company was hindered in 1939 due to the Second World War, forcing cuts to services and the complete dropping of non-essential work. However, there was growth in some services where additional buses were needed to support industries with a shift towards double-deckers, which continued in peacetime.

In 1942 the T&BAT was split into its constituent groups of British Electric Traction (BET) Company Ltd and Tilling Motor Services Ltd, with Crosville coming under the latter. By 1945 Tilling green had replaced the maroon fleet livery previously adopted by LMS, with Tilling-owned Bristol vehicles favoured.

As the company continued to expand, management changes also took place. On 31 March 1945 Claude Crosland Taylor died at the young age of forty-five, having headed the company since 1923 following the death of his father. Following Claude's passing his brother James was appointed the company's general manager, continuing the family connection with the company.

By the end of the Second World War, Crosville found itself in a very healthy position. Over 50 per cent more passengers were now being carried and revenue was up almost 90 per cent compared with that pre-war. As a result, the company was able to reinvest in property which would rise in value. Post-war service provision grew once more as additional resources became available in the form of driving staff and vehicles.

A 1937 Crosville advert promoting its many services. (Crosville Motor Services)

13

3
Edge Lane Depot

In the early years it had always been Crosville's ambition to access the lucrative bus market of Liverpool and the company was proactively looking for ways to enter the city. The Crosland Taylors identified Warrington and Widnes as possible access points. In June 1922 the company introduced three new routes from an outstation in Widnes that would serve Speke, Garston and Warrington. However, this was subsequently closed when a new depot was opened on Chester New Road, Warrington, in 1923.

Up until 1925, Liverpool City Council had refused access to the city centre by all private bus operators, but allowed Crosville to set up a new terminus at Canning Place when an agreement was reached with Ribble Motor Services.

Having successfully sought permission, in August 1925 the company extended its Widnes to Garston bus service on an hourly basis to Canning Place. This was, however,

An aerial view of Crosville's Edge Lane depot, Liverpool, in 1952.

subject to an agreement not to carry local passengers within the city boundary unless they paid a minimum fare of 6d.

In 1927 the company purchased land in Liverpool at the junction of Church Road and Edge Lane measuring 3,350 square yards. Here what would become known as the company's Edge Lane depot would be built and brought into use in June 1928. Additional adjoining land was purchased in 1937, with maintenance facilities being extended in 1942.

In 1929 the company introduced its first regular daily service between Liverpool and London with four twenty-five-seat Leyland Tiger coaches, with registration FM 5222 to FM 5225 and fleet numbers 175 to 178. Routes to Chester and North Wales were introduced from Liverpool in the 1930s.

Edge Lane was not only a bus depot with maintenance facilities but also a coach station for long-distance services.

Crosville's Liverpool to London coach service timetable leaflet from 1930. (Crosville Motor Services)

Crosville's Edge Lane depot engineering shed extension.

The company continued to operate and thrive across Liverpool and the wider region as additional depots were opened and services were further developed.

By 1929 Crosville had an operating area covering the Wirral and into Lancashire, in addition to operating services in Cheshire and North and Mid Wales. By 1930 this was consolidated with many other smaller companies acquired by the company in its attempt to dispel competition.

Crosville was keen to establish services between Merseyside and North Wales as the North Wales coast was rapidly becoming a popular tourist destination. In 1931 Crosville began working with Maxways and the Wirral Transport Company, two independent operators based in Birkenhead, to provide services from Liverpool, and Birkenhead to Rhyl, Colwyn Bay, Llandudno and Caernarfon.

By 1934 both operators left the arrangement to Crosville, leaving the company as the operator that would continue to run Merseyside to North Wales services.

Transport Act 1947

On 1 January 1948 the Transport Act 1947 came into effect. It nationalised the railway network, long-distance road haulage, canals, sea, shipping ports and bus companies under the administration of the British Transport Commission (BTC), which acquired the Tilling Group shareholding. At the same time the Railway Executive took control of the four mainline railway companies with their shareholding in Crosville passing over to the BTC.

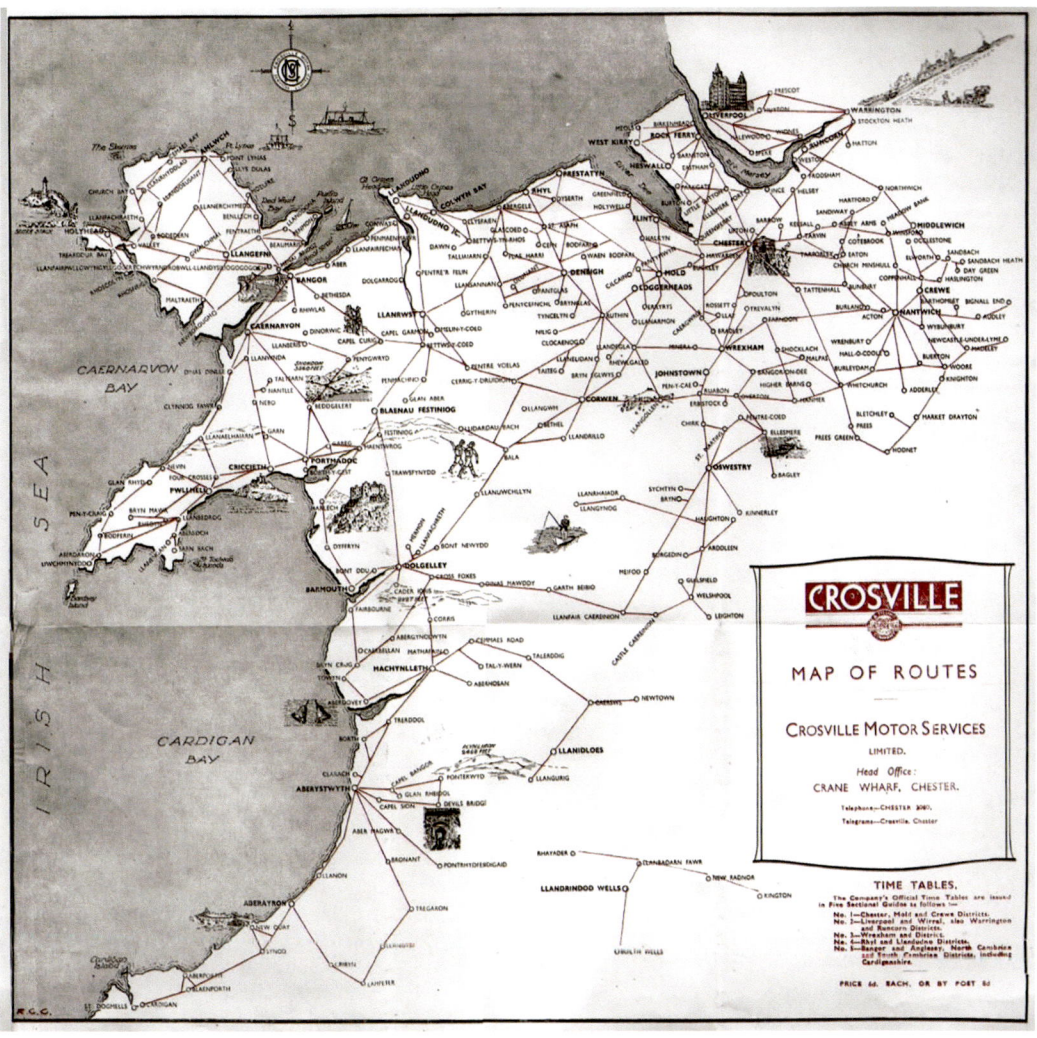

Crosville's network map from 1948. (Crosville Motor Services)

Crosville in the same way as other transport companies became state owned.

The BTC was part of a highly ambitious scheme to create a publicly owned, centrally planned, integrated transport system. In theory, the BTC was to coordinate different modes of transport, to co-operate and supplement each other instead of competing. This was to be achieved by means of fare and rate adjustments but, in practice, very little integration between modes ever materialised.

Having been a member of the Tilling Group since 1932, for a number of years almost all new buses purchased by Crosville were manufactured by the Bristol Tramways Carriage Co. with bodywork provided by Eastern Coach Works (ECW) at Lowestoft. This was a long-term effect of nationalisation.

In the 1950s staff recruitment became difficult for Crosville and other companies, leading to staff shortages as bus work at the time was relatively low paid. A one-person

Crosville United, the company's staff magazine from 1964, introducing the new impressive CRG class (ECW/Bristol RELH) of coach for the Liverpool–London service from Edge Lane depot. CRG495 and CRG496 are seen parked at Pier Head, Liverpool. (Crosville Motor Services)

DKB644 at Pier Head Liverpool on 27 May 1966. (Dave Cousins)

operation would, however, be introduced during the following decade, which would reduce labour costs in contrast with the traditional driver and conductor model.

During the 1960s Crosville adopted a contraction policy that involved withdrawing from unprofitable routes, whilst the company was able to expand in other areas when markets supported this.

Fifteen years later, under the Transport Act 1962, the government dissolved the British Transport Commission and created the British Railway Board to take over railway duties from 1 January 1963 and the Transport Holding Company (THC) to take over bus operations from the same date.

Transport Act 1968

On 1 January 1969 the Transport Act 1968 was introduced and predominantly brought about the creation of the National Bus Company in England and Wales. This involved the merger of the bus operating companies of the government-owned Transport Holdings Company (THC) and the British Electric Traction (BET) into a single state-owned National Bus Company (NBC).

EMG487 at Edge Lane depot, Liverpool, in January 1967. (Dave Cousins)

The main provisions of the Act made changes to the structure of nationally owned bus companies and created Passenger Transport Authorities (PTAs) and Executives (PTEs) to take over public transport coordination in large conurbations.

The National Bus Company inherited 75 per cent shareholdings in chassis-manufacturer Bristol Commercial Vehicles (BCV) and body-builder Eastern Coach Works (ECW) from the THC. Also in 1969 NBC formed a joint venture with British Leyland, who owned the other 25 per cent of Bristol and ECW, leading to the design of the Leyland National.

The Act also required local authorities to financially support non-profitable bus services and to provide for infrastructure grants for major transport projects from central government. It also supported the move towards a one-person operation away from the traditional driver and conductor with up to 25 per cent of the cost of new buses of approved design.

The Scottish Transport Group was also formed at the beginning of 1969, combining the Scottish Bus Group and Caledonian Steam Packet Company shipping line.

Many Crosville routes were declared loss-making, with councils subsidising their continuation as otherwise they would have been withdrawn. It is understood that Crosville submitted a list of nearly 200 routes that required financial assistance.

DFB113, Liverpool Edge Lane depot, January 1967. (Dave Cousins)

Some of the leaflets produced over the years by Crosville to promote its longer distance services from Liverpool to London, Cardiff and Caernarfon (North Wales). (Crosville Motor Services)

Merseyside Passenger Transport Executive

The Transport Act 1968 would make way for Passenger Transport Authorities (PTAs) that would set out transport policy and public transport expenditure plans in their regions, made up of councillors from the various local authorities within each region. The Passenger Transport Executives (PTEs) would deliver on the PTAs' strategies, as well as taking over municipal bus operators from individual councils and responsibility for managing local rail networks.

The Merseyside Passenger Transport Executive, or MPTE for short, was established on 1 December 1969 along with the Merseyside Passenger Transport Authority. The latter included representation from eighteen different councils and would become responsible for the day-to-day operations of transport services in the region, including policy and strategy.

Other such authorities were introduced across the UK: West Midlands on 1 October 1969; South East Lancashire North East Cheshire (SELNEC) on 1 November 1969; Tyneside on 1 January 1970; and Greater Glasgow on 1 June 1973.

The formation of the MPTE meant that Crosville services would become a part of the overall bus network within Liverpool. This had little impact initially on Crosville but it changed traditional Crosville routes later in the 1970s.

Above: Crosville G118 (KFM 767) parked outside the company's Edge Lane depot on 23 May 1970. It had been converted into a tow bus in 1967. The vehicle's original fleet number as a bus was KG 118 of 1950 build. The vehicle is in preservation at the time of writing. (John Lee)

Below: SRG220 on service H22 from Liverpool to Chester outside Widnes town hall on 20 May 1972. (Dave Cousins)

Following the introduction of the Local Government Act 1972, in 1974 the MPTE's boundaries extended over the same area as the new metropolitan county of Merseyside and was made up of twenty-three councillors of the new Merseyside County Council. The MPTE would also operate a large proportion of the bus services on Merseyside under the Merseyside Transport brand, having taken over municipally provided bus services of Birkenhead, Liverpool and Wallasey corporation in 1970. In 1974 operations were expanded to cover St Helens and Southport.

Not only had the PTE a co-ordination role, but they were operators of the former Liverpool Corporation routes. Bus services in Merseyside were provided by MPTE, Crosville and Ribble.

The National Bus Company

The National Bus Company (NBC) was formed from the Transport Act 1968 on 1 January 1969 and would operate in England and Wales. It would not operate bus services directly itself but would become the owner of regional subsidiary companies such as Crosville. It would be responsible for group policy and strategic decisions, as well as the establishment of a uniform national brand that would be applied across all of its subsidiary companies.

CRL299 at Crosville's Liverpool Edge Lane depot on 16 March 1975 in the NATIONAL white coaching livery. (Dave Cousins)

Frederick (Freddie) Wood was appointed NBC chairman in 1972 and under his leadership it moved to bring together all of the scheduled coach services operated by its subsidiary companies under the Central Activities Group and under one network brand from the same year onwards. It would also include holiday tours and the development of special services. Each region would have a director who would report to the chief executive and management board.

A new corporate identity would be launched on 10 April 1972, replacing traditional liveries and identities of subsidiary companies. Coaches would be identified by an all-white livery with the word 'NATIONAL' displayed each side of the vehicle in alternate red and blue letters. Buses used on local bus services would adopt a uniform design of a single colour, based on their traditional house colours. Green and red were generally used, and in the minority blue and yellow.

At the heart of this new identity would be a new logo created by designer Norman Wilson, consisting of a sloping red letter 'N', with mirrored blue 'N' underneath, creating a double 'N' arrow effect. This would be a truly iconic logo that would become synonymous with NBC buses and coaches.

Crosville Bristol Lodekkas in the NBC bus livery at Mann Island on a rainy day in March 1980. (Robert J. Montgomery)

ENL827 in the NBC dual-purpose livery is seen at the Wavetree Clock Tower on 28 February 1985. The late David Knipe is at the wheel. (Robert J. Montgomery)

Semi-bus/coach (dual-purpose) vehicles would appear in the typical green or red livery but with the vehicle's upper half painted white.

The NBC by then was a £100 million organisation with far-reaching plans to revitalise everyday bus services. This included the creation of its national intercity passenger road transport service.

Freddie Wood, the new NBC chairman, summed up his new policy in one sentence: 'My objective for N.B.C. is that we should be able to provide those members of the public who want it with a good, reliable road transport service and make a profit for the nation in doing so.'

Every effort was made by the NBC to promote the new identity across its subsidiaries. In the early years of the NBC, there was some rationalisation, generally leading to the amalgamation of operators into larger units and the transfer of areas between them. Crosville would take over depots in Lampeter, Newcastle Emlyn and New Quay in Wales from Western Welsh.

From October 1973 Crosville lost control of its express services with management passing to National Travel (North West) Ltd, Manchester, the renamed dormant North Western Road Car Company Ltd. The Crosville chart room based at Crosville's Edge Lane depot was subsequently relocated to Ribble's Skelhorne Street station opposite Lime Street railway station. Each NBC subsidiary would create supporting literature and publicity promoting the NBC.

25

NATIONAL BUS COMPANY
REORGANISED
NEW LOOK FOR NATION-WIDE COACH SERVICES

Freddie Wood, the new Chairman of the National Bus Company, announced today that the £100 million organisation has been given a new policy and a new look. Far-reaching plans have been made to revitalise the everyday bus services and to create a national inter-city passenger road transport service.

Mr. Wood, who became chairman of the National Bus Company at the beginning of the year, today held his first Press conference and disclosed his plans for the future. Also on view for the first time was a National coach in its bright new livery—white with red and blue lettering and symbol.

He explained that in the three months since he had become chairman and Jim Skyrme had been appointed chief executive, extensive changes had been made. England and Wales has been divided into three regions (east, west and south). A separate Central Group had been set up responsible for national express services, holiday tours and the development of special services, each with a director reporting to the chief executive and the management board.

Mr. Wood summed up his policy in one sentence: "My objective for N.B.C. is that we should be able to provide those members of the public who want it with a good, reliable road transport service and make a profit for the nation in doing so."

His strategy is two-pronged:

1. Stage-carriage still constitutes the vast bulk of our traffic and earnings. We propose to maintain and improve our service in this area by whatever means at our disposal, specifically including vital and energetic management and methods, marketing, economies and rationalisation.

2. We intend vigorously to develop all other legitimate areas of growth in public transport to which our assets in human resources and equipment can be applied. Specifically we will expand on a national basis inter-city services, holiday tours and possibly develop into travel agency and other allied activities.

Mr. Wood continued: "The bus remains throughout the world the most flexible and adaptable means of moving people about in large numbers. Old services can easily be varied and new services simply provided due to the availability of all the necessary ingredients, i.e., the track in the form of the road, the buses, the drivers and the organisation.

"And, as the campaigns by successive governments against the private car proceed, the bus must eventually come into its own.

"There is a prodigious amount of talent in N.B.C. Our human resources in terms of management and labour are very real and very considerable.

"We have excellent engineering facilities, maintenance centres, bus depots and much real estate capable of considerable development.

"We are adequately capitalised for our needs (if we accept the rather quaint debt structure in which we work under the Exchequer).

"The great bulk of our business (say 85%) is still in stage-carriage. We must therefore continue to maintain pressure in this main area. It will, for the time being at least, continue to be operated on a company basis, although of course, we shall continue the policy of merging companies where appropriate. The traditional names will continue although all companies' liveries will embrace a common national emblem.

"We must ceaselessly pursue all possible avenues of profitable services in this area. We must examine mini-bus operations in country areas. We must consider the possibility of increasing our involvement in the carriage of parcels, possibly jointly with the Post Office and the National Freight Corporation. We see a role for the rural bus as the village carrier for some areas.

"We must find what the customer wants and provide his requirements at a profit.

"I believe that, in a few years, enough pressure from governments here and abroad will bring counter-legislation against the car which will bring the bus into its own. But we shall be realistic and assume that it will not happen for the next few years and until then the car will continue its relentless progress.

"In which case, we may well be faced with further declines in passengers on stage-fare business however hard we try to fulfil the public's requirements.

"The answer to many of our problems will, I hope be found in the achievements of the Central Activities Group. It has a number of divisions, of which the first two are: (1) Inter-city express coach operations; and (2) Holiday tours.

"I believe that national express coach operations is an area where we can give a necessary and popular service to part of the public. This is a growth area where we can work profitably. I visited Greyhound in the States last year and some of my thinking on Express has been influenced by experience there. At any rate, we propose to follow broadly the recommendations of a recent research report, which run briefly as follows:

(a) All Express operations of N.B.C. companies will be run as one service under one management as a division of the Central Activities Group.

(b) There will be a common livery displaying a common brand name for all the coaches concerned, common working systems and tickets.

(c) Companies concerned with coaching will be absorbed into the Central Activities Group, and the coaches of stage-carriage bus companies that at present run express coach services will be allocated to the Central Group, although bus companies will continue to own, maintain and operate the vehicles.

"Holiday tours, at present marketed by 16 N.B.C. subsidiary companies, is a potentially profitable area which we shall operate in future as a centrally controlled function.

"Our network of booking offices suggests that there may be good grounds for us considering a national chain of travel agencies. There are other areas that we shall be exploring as the months pass.

"Our policy, therefore, is to continue to press the traditional stage-carriage business through the three new regional groups and to apply new and strong effort on our centralised activities."

Crosville United, spring 1972, issue 80, introducing the new-look National wide coach services to Crosville staff. (Crosville Motor Services)

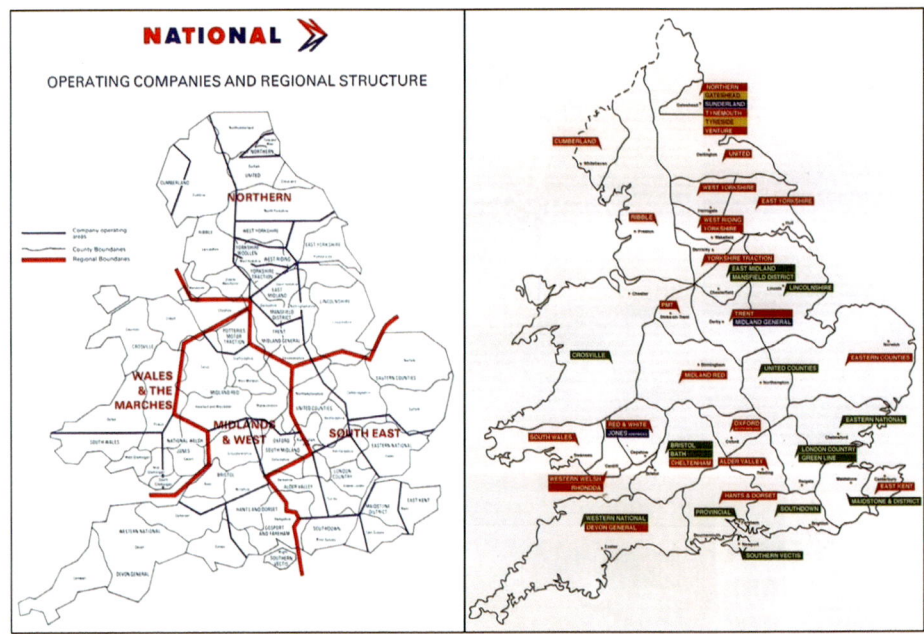

Official NBC maps showing regional structure and operating companies. (National Bus Company)

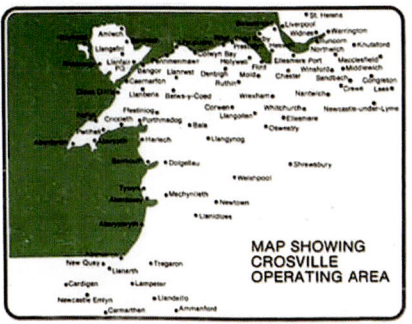

A typical NBC subsidiary produced leaflet promoting the fact that Crosville was now a part of the NATIONAL bus company.

Professional and Proud

Crosville's Edge Lane depot was home to many professional staff members who took pride in their work.

Not only did Crosville provide local bus services in and around Liverpool and long-distance scheduled coach services, but also private hire, ranging from one coach to many. As an example, Crosville would supply coaches for the annual biennial BICC staff outing. It was a prestigious and major logistical exercise for the company involving the transportation of around 2,000 people, all by forty-six Crosville coaches.

Crosville's Edge Lane depot at the time was a hive of coaching activity, operating the Liverpool to London services, North Wales, Cardiff and other long-distance routes. To illustrate the scale of the operation during the winter alone, there were three journeys a day to London, one via the motorways, a daytime service using only A roads, which took around eleven hours, and an overnight service, Mike Lambden recalls. Two journeys a day would operate to Caernarfon and one to Llandudno at this time.

In 1972 the CRL class of vehicle was introduced for the Liverpool to London coach services. These were the Series 2, Mark 2 Bristol RELH/ECW-bodied coaches, powered by the Leyland 0.680 engine. They were much faster than the elegant CRGs powered by the solid and very reliable but slower Gardner engines and improved service journey times.

Crosville's Liverpool Edge Lane depot staff about to embark on a long-service outing during 1970. Standing in front of a CRG class coach, the group includes, left to right: Harry Parry (conductor on the North Wales services), Tommy Leech (garage driver and former express driver), Harry Wood (London driver), Harry Draper (London driver), Bob Parry (London driver), Jack Cowap (London driver), Sid Green (London driver), Les Brereton (DTS Liverpool and ex-London driver), Jimmy Corbett (engineering charge hand), Alan Plews (ticket inspector), Billy Lawson (engineering supervisor), Dennis Revill (garage foreman), Bob Campbell (depot inspector), Hugh Whitby (London driver), Sam Thompson (conductor who worked the Capenhurst contract), Bert Drew (driver and union chairman) and Syd Bird (London driver). (Mike Lambden)

Immaculately turned out CRG coaches on the 1970 BICC outing lined up on Manchester Road, Prescot. Nine CRGs and five CMGs were provided by Edge Lane depot. (Mike Lambden)

Coach number 6 leaves Prescot station at the start of the journey to Blackpool, with the local constabulary on hand to control traffic. (Mike Lambden)

CRG162 is seen at the rear of Crosville's Edge Lane depot having returned from London on 23 May 1970. (John Lee)

CRG110 at Edge Lane depot in the early 1970s. The group includes Les Brereton and John Valente on the step and Mike Lambden, Harold 'Ag' Thompson, Pat Taylor and Pam Carmichael at the front. (Mike Lambden)

NEW LONDON EXPRESS SERVICES

Faster journeys, more departures, new Motorway links and good Weekend facilities are all part of the new look London-Merseyside Express Coach Services introduced on 9 June, 1972.

Mr. L. Brereton, District Traffic Superintendent at Edge Lane Depot in Liverpool, wishes Driver J. Martin bon voyage prior to taking the first coach on the new Motorway Service to London. This was the 1225 departure from Edge Lane on the 9th June.

A completely new service numbered X18 has been introduced every day linking London with Chester, Ellesmere Port, Birkenhead and Liverpool, making use of the new Motorways link in the Midlands between the M6 and M1. The journey time of 4¼ hours between London and Chester is timetabled. Apart from the normal journey each day, additional journeys are scheduled at Weekends to provide some excellent Weekend facilities both to London and Merseyside. In addition, during the summer, extra journeys also operate on Saturdays and Sundays for the benefit of holidaymakers. The new service provides some excellent connections at Chester for Heswall and West Kirby as well as the whole length of the North Wales coast. It brings Llandudno, for example, within 7 hours of London by using the connectional facilities with the now renowned Cymru Coastliner.

Speed is the keynote for the revised timings on the existing Motorway Service via Runcorn. City centre to city centre timings are improved with a time of 5 hours 15 minutes between Victoria and St. John's Lane, Liverpool. The service as is customary, terminates at Edge Lane, and with a return fare of £3·40 the new facilities are proving popular. The 0900 journey from Liverpool has now been retimed to 0805 and the 1300 journey from London has been retimed to 1810, thus providing day return opportunities from Merseyside to London at a day return fare of £2·50. With the Motorways services via Chester running at other times, the selection of departures from each end is greatly increased.

The X1 service via Stratford and Oxford is also speeded up and journeys now also stop at Chelmsley Wood in both directions. In addition the overnight service also stop at Ellesmere Port to provide a brand new service from that point. Previously only the X2 summer service via Crewe, Lichfield and the M1 has called at Ellesmere Port and now the all the year round Motorway Services will give a much needed facility to this growing town.

CRG 162 calls at Ellesmere Port Bus Station on the first X18 journey to London at 1330 on 9th June.

LLANIDLOES DEPOT, 1923–1972

Saturday, 24th June, 1972, dawned as any other day this year, but to five people in the small market town of Llanidloes, Montgomeryshire, it marked the end of an era. For at 2305 hours that night when Driver S. Reamsbottom brought SMG 437 on to The Gro Bus Park it was the very last service journey to be operated by Llanidloes Depot. The Crosville establishment in Llanidloes was almost surely the smallest depot on any part of the National Bus Company's complex, for at its peak the most vehicles allocated there was four.

Crosville first arrived in Llanidloes in 1923 when they set up a small depot in a yard behind the Trewythan Arms Hotel in Great Oak Street. In those days two vehicles were used to operate the service to Newtown. For a few years a service was also operated to Llangurig, a village four miles west of Llanidloes, and said to be the Highest Village in Wales. This service was operated jointly with T. Jones and Sons, Wye Garage, Llangurig and later of New Street Garage, Llanidloes, however after only a few years, the operation by Crosville was handed over to T. Jones and Sons, who continued to operate the service until the late 1960's when it was finally withdrawn. It is interesting to note that the present service D80 Llanidloes–Trefeglwys which commenced operating in the mid 1960's covers part of a route on which T. Jones also used to operate.

22   23

An extract from *Crosville United* describing the new service from Liverpool to London introduced on 7 June 1972, operated by Edge Lane depot. (Crosville Motor Services)

30

An image that 'brims atmosphere', as described by Mike Lambden, Edge Lane's assistant superintendent at the time. CRL259 is seen at Liverpool Edge Lane's coach stands, London-bound on service X61 with Hughie Whitby behind the wheel, a long-time London driver at the depot. To the right of the coach is Snowie Allen, who was the private hire officer at Liverpool, looking after coach services, with Peter Brookes second right, who later became a London driver. Third right is Brian Ford, the trade union secretary at Edge Lane depot. A CRG can be seen behind as the batten to operate the prestigious service is passed to the CRL class of coach. Mike Lambden believes that the image was taken in 1972 and is possibly the first departure on this service to be operated by a CRL class coach. This vehicle was also used in all Crosville official publicity for this class of new coach at the time. (Mike Lambden)

CRL259 (TFM 259K) on its first journey to London in 1972, with Voss Motors, Liverpool, and petrol pumps behind. Mike Lambden comments that Eric Trainer, the trade union branch chairman at the time, can be seen standing to the right of the coach. The inspector is likely to be Syd Huyton. (Mike Lambden)

Trade Union/Management Relationship

Crosville in Liverpool always had a very strong union presence. The same can be said of other industries at the time.

Bus conductors were a common sight across the UK and beyond until the late 1970s and early 1980s; Liverpool was no different. In urban areas a two-person bus crew consisting of a driver and conductor was a necessity on high-demand services operated with double-deckers. The driver would be in a separate cab, whilst the conductor dealt with passengers and fares. The conductor would communicate with the driver by way of bell pushes that would sound in the driver's cab.

The passenger entrance door would be at the rear of the vehicle, but as bus design developed in the late 1960s and 1970s this would move to the front. This eventually gave way to a one-crew-member design of what was dubbed 'one man operation', or 'OMO' for short at the time.

By the early 1980s the number of bus conductors had diminished significantly across the UK outside London. This resulted in added pressure on the bus driver, who would by now be undertaking both roles. This reduced staff resource requirement and cost significantly

DFG205 (JFM 205D) is seen at Pier Head, Mann Island, Liverpool, having operated the H3 service from Rainhill in the mid-1970s. DFG250 (SFM 250F) is parked on the right having operated service H5. (Robert J. Montgomery)

DFG249 at Warrington on the H1 to Liverpool on Saturday 8 February 1975. (Bob Downham)

less but placed intense pressure on the driver on high-use bus routes. In Liverpool the MPTE was keen to convert services to OMO as soon as possible as this would save money. However, there was a long-standing agreement between the trade union branch and Crosville management that vehicles without power steering would not be used by OMO unless volunteered.

Liverpool depot had historically operated the majority of their bus routes with double deckers due to capacity and high passenger use. Such vehicles also had standing capacity for passengers which was often utilised when buses became full. Route timetables and running times would be timed through what was called the 'running time test'. This was again a long-standing agreement between the trade union branch and management, which ensured suitable timings to the vehicles that would be used.

A number of services were very busy by their nature and by the late 1970s the 'running time test' was undertaken by the five-speed, semi-automatic Bristol VRT/ECW double-decker (DVL class) fitted with the faster Leyland engine. This type of vehicle was perfect for the faster paced routes of Liverpool. At the very worst, in accordance with the agreement, the Gardner-powered equivalent (DVG class) would be used.

There would be a number of long-standing agreements between the trade union branch and Crosville management at the Liverpool depot. Another agreement was that all vehicles

33

SRG178 is seen here parked at the rear of Edge Lane depot in August 1981. (Robert J. Montgomery)

DVL430 at Prescot on the first departure for Liverpool on the morning of Sunday 15 July 1984. (Robert J. Montgomery)

be suitably equipped with destination equipment as any driver caught by company officials operating a service without the correct destination information could face disciplinary action.

MPTE drivers in Liverpool were on better pay and working conditions than that of their Crosville counterparts with shorter duties. The trade union branch at Crosville's Liverpool depot was therefore constantly making sure that their members were not unfavourably treated in comparison.

MPTE vehicles had suitably well-designed cab doors fitted for OMO. These prevented farebox theft and were fitted with a lockable clasp, which provided speed and safety of cash fare transactions and storage for the driver. The door had a well-designed rack and dispenser with a slot to drop cash to a safe and secure area. The bottom part of the door could only be opened by the driver.

The MPTE cab door layout was designed to cope with large amounts of cash that could be scooped off the cash tray into a drawer quickly by the driver through a slot at the end, which also held the quick change device. It also had a large pull-open drawer to hold cash money bags, which was not visible to passengers. The door was made from aluminium and was a wider, much sturdier door than the standard cab door fitted.

Crosville vehicles outside Liverpool had the standard 'begging bowls', as they were called by some of the drivers, which comprised a simple tray fitted to the top of the standard cab door. Passengers placed their money on the tray in exchange for their journey ticket. A row of four cash trays was fitted inside the driver's cab door, which wasn't lockable and was visible to passengers on some vehicles due to the low height of the door. As Liverpool routes would take a lot of money such a cab door wasn't suitable because it didn't have anywhere to safeguard large sums of cash when driving bar that of the driver's jacket pockets or bag.

To the trade union branch it was a case of safety first in protecting drivers and farebox revenue, and considered only fair that Crosville's Liverpool depot had the MPTE-type door fitted to its vehicles in the same way. This underpinned another long-standing agreement at the Liverpool depot.

Crosville's Edge Lane fleet would have MPTE cab doors as standard for many years, as Bill Barlow recalls, and were identical to the cab doors fitted to MPTE buses. All Leyland National and Bristol VR buses allocated to Liverpool had their standard Crosville doors and change-giving equipment replaced by MPTE cab doors and change-givers. Quite a number of ENLs and SNLs spent their whole lives at Liverpool and never had any other style of cab door.

Another long-standing agreement at the depot was that specific staff would fuel and park up buses when drivers returned to the depot at the end of their duty.

Many have commented that Crosville's Edge Lane depot was a professional, proud and happy place with a good community spirit, with many social events taking place at the Edge Lane Hotel opposite the depot.

In the same way, across the country, long-standing agreements between the trade union and bus company management would need to be modified in the face of deregulation. Significant pressures would quickly develop on all sides during 1986 and beyond that would ultimately undermine the industrial relations between the trade union and Crosville management.

Fleet Size

Crosville's Edge Lane depot had the largest fleet of buses and coaches of any other Crosville depot in June 1979, totalling 110 buses and coaches, supported by a company van, recovery vehicle and training bus.

At this time Edge Lane depot had an impressive number of coaches/semi-coaches, totalling forty-one, and a large fleet of double-deckers, totalling forty-eight, as well as twenty-one single-deckers and three auxiliary support vehicles.

Since 1910, Crosville had developed various means of quickly identifying vehicles for internal maintenance and traffic allocation purposes within its large fleet. This initially involved naming vehicles. In 1915 this was changed to consecutively numbering each new additional vehicle to the fleet. In 1934 an alpha-digit numeric system was introduced before an alpha-numeric system was introduced in 1958. This final system saw each vehicle being recognised through a series of letters and numbers. The first letter corresponded with the vehicle type, such as a coach (C); a dual-purpose express coach (E); a double-decker (D); a high-bridge double-decker (H); and a single-deck vehicle (S).

The second letter corresponded to the vehicle's chassis, i.e. for a Bristol Lodekka or Leyland Leopard (L); Leyland National (N); Bristol RE (R); and a Bristol VRT (V).

Crosville's official 'Vehicle Allocation Summary Sheet' from 1 June 1979. Liverpool Edge Lane depot is listed as 'LP'. (Crosville Motor Services)

London driver Jack Cowap standing in front of Leyland Leopard CLL333 at Edge Lane depot on 16 September 1980. (Bill Barlow)

The third letter corresponded to the vehicle's engine, i.e. Bristol (B); Gardner (G); and Leyland (L). The fleet number would normally correspond to the registration number of the vehicle, but this was not always the case if the same numbers were already in use within the fleet. For example, DVL359 would be a double-decker (D) Bristol VR (V) powered by a Leyland engine (L); registration YTU 359S.

In keeping with this system of vehicle recognition within the company, the type of vehicles used on services and allocated to Edge Lane depot in June 1979 were: fourteen CLLs; one remaining CRG; twenty CRLs; nine DFGs; thirteen DVGs; twenty-six DVLs; one EPG; five ENLs; eight SNL 'A's; and thirteen SRGs.

The SNL 'A' was the first production Leyland National which was an integrally modular constructed vehicle, developed as a joint project between the NBC and British Leyland and built in 1972.

The coaching complement at Edge Lane depot would reduce from this point as vehicles would be redistributed to other company depots to operate Town Lynx-branded express services, which commenced in 1979, as well as the introduction of the National Travel West unit in 1980.

By 1984 Liverpool depot's average peak vehicle requirement (PVR) was 46.7 buses, the H6 route (Liverpool–Prescot) being the highest at 10.4.

37

DVG275 at Crosville's Edge Lane depot in 1981. It features special branding celebrating seventy-five years of Crosville from 1906 to 1981. (Les A. Smith)

Market Analysis Project

The Viable Network Project started at Midland Red in 1976, before expanding to other operators and becoming NBC group policy. It was renamed the Market Analysis Project, or MAP for short, commencing at Crosville in May 1978.

Originally it was confined to Wales, but adopted across England when Cheshire abandoned its own review project, as Andrew Cudbertson, Crosville's Planning Manager at the time, recalls. He remembers a former Bristol Omnibus Lodekka, fleet number G775 (223 NAE) kitted out as Crosville's MAP project bus, populated by numbers of surveyors and support staff to undertake the project.

Passenger demand for local services was in decline at this time, with costs rising fast. Ever-increasing car ownership and record inflation in 1975 were also significant, so that by the end of 1976 passengers carried outside London were 20 per cent down on 1970 levels. As a consequence, blanket network support requested of local authorities was increasing year by year. MAP's purpose was to identify passenger demand and more clearly demonstrate to operators those services and areas that could support themselves, and to local authorities where the public purse was being directed. Better use of vehicle resources, improved route planning and marketing were all features of the project, as well as making operating economies. In a sense it was a forerunner of planning for deregulation. Most importantly, this was a systematic area by area review for all NBC companies, not just a reaction to a crisis.

Andrew Cudbertson recalls that the project was very much ahead of its time with the information being gathered. Passengers boarding and alighting bus services stop to stop

Above and below: Crosville's Edge Lane depot, April 1983. Robert Montgomery comments that they provide a view of almost the whole frontage of the Liverpool depot, looking eastward, nearly to the top of Edge Lane. Robert doesn't recall why ENL843 came to be facing out of the depot's entrance. (Robert J. Montgomery)

would be counted on every timetabled journey at least once on weekdays and weekends. This would be supplemented by on bus surveys that would ask for origins and destinations of passengers for analysis later into coarse and fine zones. In each survey team there would be one person undertaking the head counts whilst another would hand out and collect back the self-completed forms from passengers. Survey results would be coded and then fed into mainframe computers located in Midland House, Birmingham, before long reports were produced and sent back for error-checking and final completion.

In context, farebox revenue would also be analysed including service performance and costs incurred with a view to improving efficiency and lowering the subsidy burden on local authorities.

Once the data for services had been fully analysed, changes to services began to be implemented in the late 1970s to early 1980s. It also resulted in regional branding and stronger identity for local services and increased marketing to promote bus services and increase patronage.

Transport Act 1980

On 6 October 1980 services with journeys of 30 miles or more were deregulated under the Transport Act 1980, ending the licensing regulation imposed on express coach routes and tours over such mileage.

The late Peter Rusk is seen here washing his car at the rear of Edge Lane depot on 6 August 1977. The scale of the depot's coaching operation is clearly visible. (Bill Barlow)

This resulted in the introduction of competition between publicly owned companies such as National Express and subsidiaries of Scottish Bus Group (SBG) and privately owned companies. The Act also allowed authorities to set up 'trial areas' that would deregulate bus services on a trial basis.

In preparation for the new regime, National Travel West was set up at Skelhorne Street in Liverpool during 1980. It would be a new standalone NBC-owned coaching unit, which would draw vehicles and staff from Crosville and Ribble.

Crosville's contribution involved five Duple Leyland Leopards, CLL321 to CLL325 (YTU 321S to YTU 325S), built in 1977. A number of long-standing drivers from Edge Lane depot transferred to this new unit on a snowy Sunday 23 March 1980. This took a huge amount of work out of the depot and the progression of drivers to 'big wheel', as it was known. This was a big loss to Crosville and Edge Lane depot.

Graham Warren remembers his dad George Warren at the time commenting that, 'When the coaches go, Edge Lane will go.'

CLL324 in the all-over NATIONAL white coaching livery, parked at the rear of Crosville's Edge Lane depot in May 1979. (Robert J. Montgomery)

4

Crosville Liverpool in Photographs

Inside Edge Lane depot with the inspector's mini, registration NDM 112Y, on the left in July 1984. (Robert J. Montgomery)

Above: Jimmy Riley, Lol Doyle and Dougie Thom at Mann Island Pier Head in October 1984. (Robert J. Montgomery)

Right: Ali Kechil on the entrance step of DVL342 at Mann Island, 16 September 1984. (Robert J. Montgomery)

Above: Edge Lane depot on 9 February 1985. The duty foreman's office can be seen on the left and the garage foreman's office on the right, with the bus wash far right. (Robert J. Montgomery)

Below: Joe Graham standing in front of CRL308 at Edge Lane depot on 16 March 1980. (Bill Barlow)

Above: Crosville's Edge Lane depot maintenance shed on 8 July 1984. It was situated to the front right of the depot's main entrance when looking from the road. (Robert J. Montgomery)

Below: Edge Lane depot's vehicle fuelling bay and bus wash in April 1985. (Robert J. Montgomery)

Above: SNL893 and ERL309 parked at the rear of Edge Lane depot in April 1985. (Robert J. Montgomery)

Left: Dave Shiels and Raymond Patterson at the fuel pumps at Edge Lane depot, July 1984. Raymond started with Crosville at Edge Lane in June 1970 as a seasonal conductor, then driver before becoming the trade union branch chairman at Crosville Liverpool from 1976 until the closure of Love Lane depot. (Robert J. Montgomery)

Right: The late George Warren, 'one of the great characters of Liverpool garage', who started with Crosville at Edge Lane in 1963 and remained with the company until the closure of Love Lane. Here he is outside the duty foreman's office at Edge Lane on 8 July 1984. Ray Jump is just about visible inside. George particularly enjoyed the North Wales express services from Liverpool, and had a difficult choice to make when National Express routes moved to Skelhorne Street in 1980. (Robert J. Montgomery)

Below: John Embleton, who started with Crosville at Edge Lane on 16 November 1970 as a conductor, then two-man crew, one-man driver, garage driver and then an inspector and any other duties he was called upon to undertake. John comments that this covered almost everything about the business. (John Embleton)

Above: John Embleton behind the wheel of HDL929 at the International Garden Festival on 28 August 1984. (Bill Barlow)

Below: Les A. Smith (baby A. B.) at Mann Island, Liverpool, on 16 September 1984. (Robert J. Montgomery)

Above: From inside the depot looking across to the rear parking area we see DVG282 and other double-deckers on 9 February 1985. (Robert J. Montgomery)

Below: DVG281 and DVL359 are seen at the rear of Edge Lane on Sunday 9 February 1985. (Robert J. Montgomery)

L322, Edge Lane depot's auxiliary breakdown/tow truck, is seen on the left parked at the rear of Edge Lane depot on 2 August 1985. This was once a North Western coach before being modified for auxiliary work. (Robert J. Montgomery)

Four Bristol VRs seen at Edge Lane depot. Robert Montgomery comments: 'Four of Edge Lane's Bristol VRs, on Saturday 3 August 1985, the day before the move to Love Lane: DVL389, DVG278, and DVL394, with one unknown.' (Robert J. Montgomery)

5
Edge Lane Depot Closure

Edge Lane depot's infrastructure had become costly to maintain by the 1980s, although repairs had been carried out on it in the 1960s and 1970s. There were also costs associated with daily vehicle light mileage between the depot and Mann Island, which was about 3 miles. There was also a time element with this as buses would be taken out from their scheduled working day for repairs or routine inspections.

Crosville's Edge Lane depot is seen here from the opposite side of the road on 3 August 1985. This would be the last day of Crosville's operations from Edge Lane before moving to its new depot at Love Lane. Robert Montogmery comments: 'DVL343 and a Northern vehicle await refuelling. Only about ten other buses were still here on site on the Saturday afternoon.' (Robert J. Montgomery)

In the mid-1970s the company established an engineering support site closer to the centre of Liverpool at Wapping (Salthouse) and then later in Maddrell Street in the early 1980s. Vehicles signed off with faults at Mann Island would be driven by Johnny Jones, the shunt driver, for repair, minimising light mileage and time out of service. Light mechanical running repairs and vehicle inspections would be carried out during the day, which saved vehicles from being removed for lengthy periods of time during the working day.

Additional parking was also available on the opposite side of the road to Edge Lane depot, where buses were parked overnight due to a lack of capacity within the depot itself. This and engineering sites closer to Mann Island only added to the depot's overall overhead costs. Remaining at Edge Lane also prohibited any expansion of operational capacity if that became necessary.

By now the coach stands at Edge Lane depot were redundant as long-distance coach services were operating to/from Skelhorne Street coach station in the centre of Liverpool, next to Lime Street railway station. There was therefore a need to consolidate operations, land and maintenance support for logistical and cost reasons.

Furthermore, in 1984 a white paper titled 'Buses' was published by the government. This set out fundamental proposals for the way buses would be run outside Greater London and across the UK in the coming years. The proposal was to deregulate bus services outside

The view from Crosville's Edge Lane depot to the overflow bus park on the opposite side of the road on 9 February 1985. (Robert J. Montgomery)

Redundant coach stands at Edge Lane depot with training bus G166 (former DFG166) on 2 August 1985. Robert Montgomery comments: 'A very different scene from summer Saturdays back in the 1960s and 1970s.' (Robert J. Montgomery)

Greater London and privatise state-owned subsidiaries of the National Bus Company, and reduce public subsidies. If introduced, it could have had a significant impact on Crosville. Reducing overhead costs was therefore a necessity for the company.

On Saturday 3 August 1985, Edge Lane depot closed with the company's operations relocated to a new depot at the end of Love Lane, Liverpool, from Sunday 4 August.

53

Keith Cox is seen here on the last day of operations at Edge Lane depot in front of DVL359 on Saturday 3 August 1985. (Robert J. Montgomery)

Robert J. Montgomery is seen here in front of the camera for once, behind the wheel of DVL364 on Saturday 3 August 1985, driving past Edge Lane depot on its final day of operations. (The late Peter Rusk)

By 5 February 1986 heavy machinery was on site at Edge Lane, tearing down the depot. Robert Montgomery comments: 'The depressing scene at Edge Lane depot, Liverpool, six months after closure. Demolition of the long shed fronting on to the main road is well under way with the booking office next.' (Robert J. Montgomery)

6

Love Lane Depot

The old Tate & Lyle site at the end of Love Lane, which closed down on 22 April 1981 as a part of the company's rationalisation scheme, would be chosen as the new site for Crosville's depot in Liverpool. It had ample parking as well as maintenance facilities and supporting infrastructure on site and only about 1.3 miles to the north from Pier Head.

Love Lane would be a rented site from the Merseyside Docks and Harbour Co., and provided Crosville with the opportunity of moving depots relatively quickly. The company's future beyond deregulation was uncertain at this point and this was a leap into the unknown.

Love Lane depot viewed from a passing train. (Geoff O'Brien)

Geoff O'Brien behind the wheel of HVG932 on the Garden Festival service in May 1984. (Geoff O'Brien)

The new depot had a compliment of 270 staff, 230 of whom were drivers, with the remaining forty made up of engineering, local management, administrative, clerical and other staff.

The fleet at Liverpool depot now totalled seventy vehicles plus one towing vehicle, having reduced in number from the 110 previously noted at Edge Lane in 1979. Three dual-purpose coaches remained, which were ELL320, ERL305 and ERL309, branded in the Town Lynx venetian-blind variant of the livery.

Geoff O'Brien remembers starting with Crosville at Edge Lane as a conductor two weeks after decimalisation on 15 February 1971, before becoming a driver in early 1973 and trade union shop steward in the mid-1970s.

Geoff remembers Love Lane being a happy depot initially in the same way as Edge Lane. He recalls that the depot's operations were very efficient with enough vehicles and drivers to operate all services, meeting all long-term standing agreements established between the trade union and Crosville management.

However, all this would change at deregulation.

The Transport Act 1985

Due to decreasing bus patronage since the 1950s and the level of supporting bus subsidies, the Conservative government elected in 1979 was keen to adopt a new approach in the way buses would be run outside Greater London. Their intention was to reduce subsidies,

Ken Robinson, the late Neil Goodheart and Melvyn Robinson at Mann Island in May 1985. Ken and Melvyn are the sons of the late Frank Robinson, who also worked for Crosville at Liverpool and was respected by all who knew him. (Robert J. Montgomery)

introduce competition and privatise state-owned bus companies. It was argued that this would improve passenger experience by making buses and trains more efficient. The government was committed to reducing public expenditure. A white paper titled 'Buses' was published in 1984 with supportive, more detailed consultation papers setting out proposals to deregulate local buses outside Greater London in the UK.

Buses in London were governed by the London Regional Transport Act 1984, which transferred responsibility for the bus network from the Greater London Council to London Regional Transport, which would result in the establishment of London Buses in 1985.

Following the legislative process, the Transport Act 1985 was first published on 19 December 1985, to be enacted from 26 October 1986, which would be dubbed deregulation day. It would introduce the greatest change in the way bus services would operate in the UK for a long time. In essence it would replace publicly owned bus operators and highly regulated bus services with a competitive, deregulated and privatised system. It was intended that through competition costs would be driven down.

The main legal changes that would be introduced through the Transport Act 1985 can be summarised as follows:

- The abolition of route licensing, creating a deregulated free competitive bus market.
- The introduction of a new system of registration, allowing bus companies to commence, vary or cancel local bus services by giving the statutory notice period to Traffic Commissioners.
- Removing the duties of local authorities to coordinate public passenger transport.

- Withdrawal of the block grant funding previously provided by local government to bus companies to cover losses and replacing it with powers to local authorities to support specific unprofitable services which were deemed socially necessary through competitive bus tenders.
- Low fare polices were made illegal with the Traffic Commissioner's role of fare setting being removed.
- The privatisation of NBC's subsidiary companies, shifting the major cost and responsibility of bus service delivery from public ownership to the private sector.
- Local authorities would be given discretionary powers to provide concessionary travel for elderly and disabled groups.
- Municipal bus departments were reconstituted as arms-length companies to be governed by company law.

Preparing for Deregulation

The Transport Act 1985 would set the scene for what would play out for Crosville in 1986 and beyond. It would also be the case for other similar state-owned subsidiary companies of the NBC in the build-up to deregulation and subsequent privatisation. Crosville would be forced to prepare for a number of significant challenges.

DVL393 parked outside the traffic office of Love Lane depot with driver Glyn Jones alongside, about to depart. (Geoff O'Brien)

The annual agreed grants from local authorities (c. £12 million in 1985) to Crosville in exchange for operated services would cease the day before deregulation day.

For 1985 the company's secretary had quoted a profit of £2 million from a total revenue of £39.8 million for the same period. This was based on historic costing and made no allowance for replacement assets. Including replacement costs turned this profit into a loss.

Crosville had to establish which of its services could operate commercially from deregulation day and which would no longer be viable from its vast bus network. For an operation to be commercially viable, income had to be sufficient to cover the cost of operation and provide a sustainable contribution to overheads without public subsidy support.

Furthermore, the abolition of route licensing from deregulation day was likely to generate direct road competition from other operators (potentially new) for passengers and fares on Crosville routes. Under the new regime any bus operator with a valid operating licence could run a local bus service on any route once registered with the Traffic Commissioner's Office.

It would therefore be difficult for the company to work out which services were likely to be commercially viable from deregulation day and beyond. What was perceived to be potentially commercial at an early stage in a non-competitive environment could quickly become the opposite in the face of new on-road competition, especially if some services were already only marginal. In fairness to company managers, the many challenges they faced in the lead up to deregulation would be enormous and would only intensify as further pressures and targets would be placed upon them.

On 1 January 1986, the company abolished its traditional divisional management structure in favour of ten new operational districts, with existing divisional managers having to apply for the new posts, with the process only commencing in September 1985. The future of each district would depend on its financial success or otherwise post-deregulation. Liverpool, previously included with the Wirral operations, would now be a standalone district.

Determining what operations could be commercial or otherwise would involve a detailed review by the company of all of its routes to establish operating cost and income. It was clear from the outset that the company's overhead costs were high due to the portfolio of depots it possessed. The company's rationale for moving its operations from Edge Lane to Love Lane was to reduce costs. In comparison, competitor costs were likely to be lower than Crosville if they did not have large premises to maintain. Ironically, it was also likely that competitors would use cascaded older buses of little value from NBC fleets to compete. Such lower costs would be reflected through on-road competition against Crosville in fares charged, as well as lower tendering bids for contracts.

Crosville therefore had to find efficiency savings where possible to become commercially leaner and viable if the company was to stand any chance of surviving beyond deregulation and as privatisation approached.

Once routes and networks were reviewed by the company it was expected (in the same way as all other bus companies) to register those services it intended to operate commercially from deregulation day with the Office of the Traffic Commissioner between 3 and 28 February 1986, which would be published and publicly available by 1 April 1986.

Daytime urban operations were generally found to be commercial but less so for early mornings, evenings and Sundays. Liverpool to Runcorn, Liverpool to Warrington and services in Cheshire would be registered on this basis.

In total, only 56 per cent of Crosville's mileage would be registered as viable, which involved ditching 96 per cent of Sunday services and 66 per cent of early morning and evening mileage. The viable network going forward would be 48 per cent of mileage in Wales and 61 per cent in England.

Details of on-road competition following deregulation would not be available until 1 April 1986, when this information was published. Objections to any new competitive service registered could not be put forward.

After receipt of commercial intentions by the deadline date of 28 February 1986, all local authorities/PTEs had to assess transport needs in their immediate areas and seek competitive tender prices from interested bus companies to operate those not otherwise provided.

Contracting authorities had to take into account a combination of economy, efficiency and effectiveness when tendering with routes awarded to operators who could run the best service at the most cost-effective price. Contract tender specifications would specify route, service timetable and frequency, as well as other important relevant requirements.

Tendering bus operators had to be accurate in their costings and income estimations when submitting tender prices. Over pricing would lead to tenders not being won and pricing out of the market, whilst under pricing would result in contracts operating at a loss.

ELL320 in the later Town Lynx livery at Love Lane depot on 24 May 1986. (Robert J. Montgomery)

If all of this wasn't stressful enough for company management, on 13 February 1986 the Secretary of State for Transport directed that Crosville, Ribble and London Country Bus Services be split into smaller companies ahead of deregulation. The rationale was that they posed too great a competitive threat to others on deregulation at their existing size. It is believed that the minister's decision was contrary to the recommendations made by department advisors. This was only fifteen days before the deadline for companies to make their commercial intentions known to local authorities/PTE's and placed further intense pressure on company management to meet this new requirement.

Crosville Motor Services would be split into two separate companies. Crosville Motor Services Ltd would continue to operate all English-based operations from deregulation, whilst a new company in the form of Crosville Wales would be established on 20 May 1986 from the dormant Devon General Omnibus & Touring Company. It would become fully operational by 10 August 1986 and would take over Crosville Motor Services' operations in Wales, including the company's Oswestry depot.

Two separate and autonomous management structures would be set up as a part of this process from within Crosville Motor Services, both now grappling with the adverse challenges of deregulation.

Both companies also had to establish a new outward identity from deregulation beyond that of their NBC identity. Crosville Wales would adopt the colours of the Welsh National flag for its livery with a new bespoke dragon created for its logo. Crosville Motor Services

Crosville Wales SNG408 in the post-deregulation livery and branding adopted by the new company at Rhyl station on 4 September 1987. (Robert J. Montgomery)

opted for a marigold orange and brunswick green livery initially along with the leaping Lynx logo used on its Town Lynx services.

Downward variations to the commercial bus services registered in February could be done by 31 July 1986. However, proposals to reduce or withdraw services had to be supported in writing by local authorities. The deadline for registration of new services obtained since the end of February through conventional road licensing would be 13 September 1986, and the deadline for registering local bus services obtained through successful tendering or variations to increase registered services would be 25 October 1986.

Whilst Crosville feared the unknown of deregulation, it also looked at it as an opportunity to determine its own commercial services and set the fares going forward, away from the control of the MPTE.

It is understood that the award of new contracts became rushed as a result of late tender awards. This led to the trade union at Love Lane depot raising concerns about new driver duties being hurriedly produced in preparation for deregulation day, with a number of iterations made before they would be accepted. John Embleton, who worked for Crosville at Edge Lane and Love Lane depots, recalls that driver duties back then were produced by hand via pen and paper.

On 24 August 1986, two months from deregulation day, DVG274, in its traditional NBC green, is at Love Lane depot. DVL443, on the right, has adopted the company's new identity. (Robert J. Montgomery)

Local authority network support negotiated annually was about to cease. The acceptance of such profound and significant changes in the way buses would be run and funded for both company and employees would be extremely difficult and unpalatable.

1986 was a perfect storm for Crosville and events were completely outside its control, from the many requirements and deadlines imposed on it in the lead-up to deregulation. The pressure on management was intensified by the short space of time it had to prepare. Considering the new requirements, it was remarkable what management were able to achieve by deregulation day. David Meredith, Crosville's managing director, commented: 'We all have to accept that in the future we shall be living and working in a very different world from that which existed earlier this year.'

Once all services were registered ahead of deregulation, a moratorium was put in place for three months from deregulation day that would temporarily prohibit any activity in terms of service changes. Operators would be free thereafter to register, vary or cancel routes by providing the statutory notice period for any registration alterations to the Traffic Commissioner.

Also in the lead-up to deregulation the NBC had been instructed to put forward proposals to the Secretary of State within three months of the passage of the Act for the disposal and sale of its assets. It was not actively allowed to pursue privatisation until the after effects of deregulation could be measured. This was based on the assumption that companies would remain in its ownership during this period.

ENL827 and SNL876 parked side by side at Love Lane depot. (Geoff O'Brien)

MCW Metroliner Coaches for National Express

Whilst Crosville was under intense pressure, busily preparing for deregulation, May 1986 saw five new MCW double-decker coaches, registration C213 KMA to C217 KMA (CMC213–217), introduced to Liverpool Love Lane depot for use on National Express Trans Pennine services between Liverpool, Manchester, Leeds and Hull for the summer. This was a positive attempt by David Meredith, Crosville's Managing Director, to return the company to such operations and was supported by the trade union.

The service would be operated jointly between Crosville, East Yorkshire Motor Services and West Yorkshire Road Car Co., all with similar vehicles to each other. Furthermore, Crosville and East Yorkshire drivers would drive each other's vehicles to maximise efficient bus and driver workings.

Only weeks after delivery of the new coaches a deputy trade union representative from Crosville's Love Lane branch raised issues about the cab doors fitted to the East Yorkshire coaches. The branch chair and secretary were on holiday at this time.

The MCW double-deck coaches were NBC-designed. Whilst Crosville's vehicles at Liverpool were fitted with the long-standing agreement of MPTE-style cab doors and cash-taking equipment, the vehicles provided by East Yorkshire were not.

Crosville's new MCW coaches proudly lined up for use on National Express Trans Pennine services with a mix of Crosville management and drivers standing in front. (Geoff O'Brien)

As a result the trade union would not permit the East Yorkshire vehicle to be driven by Crosville staff on the rationale that a fair proportion of passenger journeys were cash fares of high value due to the type of operation. Crosville was asked by the trade union branch to agree with East Yorkshire that MPTE-style doors be fitted to their vehicles. This request was dismissed by the company, leading to strike action.

This significantly hampered the operation of the service. The MCW coaches were also the most expensive vehicles Crosville had at the time, and as such could not afford to be dragged into any disputes. Subsequently they were removed from Liverpool Love Lane depot overnight having only been there for five weeks. The vehicles and corresponding National Express work were taken over immediately the following day by Crosville's neighbouring company, Ribble, re-emerging with the Kingfisher branding.

As a result, National Express work was permanently lost at Crosville's Love Lane depot with the exception of the odd 'dupe' (duplicate) journey.

It is understood that some of the trade union representatives resigned their positions on the branch as a result. They were unhappy with the way things had transpired, having worked closely with Crosville management to bring the work to Love Lane depot in the first place.

MCW Metroliner coach Crosville CMC214 parked at Love Lane depot when new on 24 June 1986. ELL320 is seen behind. (Robert J. Montgomery)

65

Deregulation, Major Contract Wins and Closure

Deregulation on Merseyside led to Merseyside Transport being rebranded as Merseybus and privatised as Mersey Transport Ltd (MTL). The control and co-ordination of the PTE pre-deregulation was now limited to contracted services only, as Crosville and other companies established commercial operations. New operators entered the bus market, such as CMT Buses, Fareway, Liverbus, Liverline, PMT's Red Rider and others. It resulted in intense competition between operators on lucrative routes.

Ahead of deregulation during August/September 1986, the trade union branch chair for Liverpool Love Lane depot recalls being told by Crosville management that there was an urgent need to start new staff at the depot following a significant amount of bus contracts won by the company from the PTE.

The company had been successful in winning a major number of bus contracts in Liverpool from the PTE, to operate fifteen services from deregulation day, requiring twenty-three additional vehicles and 100 more drivers at Love Lane depot. This would take Liverpool depot beyond its reasonable capacity and the company outside its familiar operating territory.

Finding twenty-three additional buses and 100 new drivers would be a mammoth task for the company with such little time before deregulation. Route learning of the new services would take time as it would include all driving staff at the depot, new and old.

New routes would take the company beyond its traditional boundaries and into unfamiliar territory including housing estates. The north of Liverpool had traditionally been operated by Ribble Motor Services but now things had changed.

Separate fare levels and fare tables would be used by Crosville at different times of the day relating to commercial and tendered operations, and added pressure on drivers. There was suddenly a need to carry two different sets of paper fare scales for the same routes, reflecting different times of the day.

Whilst winning so many contracts and work was good news from deregulation for the company in one respect against tender losses suffered in other parts of the company's territory, in reality it would lead to significant pressures on the company and Love Lane depot to fulfil these.

It transpired that the tender prices submitted by Crosville to the PTE for the contracts won were too low, hence the unexpected successes leading to the need for twenty-three additional vehicles. The fares revenue risk/opportunity rested with the operator and there has been much speculation about the low contract pricing. However, no firm evidence has since come to light either to confirm the accuracy of Crosville's revenue calculations or the nature of the PTE's revenue advice given to bidders.

However, in a separate action, Crosville and North Western Road Car Co. took issue with the PTE on the fare levels set for tendered services. It appears that the PTE had imposed a cap of 15 per cent increase on tendered service bus fares in the lead-up to deregulation on 26 October 1986. Whether this affected tender pricing is not known, but the PTE were of the view that commercial fares would have to be increased by some 50 per cent in the area after deregulation. Crosville and North Western contended that lower fares on tendered services would abstract passengers from commercial services where there was an overlap on common sections of route, and this was believed to be unlawful. The long drawn-out

High Court case was finally concluded in February 1988 with an unfavourable judgement from the Court of Appeal after an original ruling by Justice Mann that detailed evidence had not been sufficiently specific. The companies decided against taking the case to the House of Lords.

It is true to say that the whole process leading up to deregulation was rushed for all concerned due to the timescales involved, as the PTE had only started inviting tenders on Friday 15 August 1986, just ten weeks before deregulation day. Crosville had never been in this situation before nor had it undertaken such an exercise, and neither had the PTE.

The low pricing of these contracts would become a major problem for Crosville from the outset, coupled with the scale of additional resources needed to operate the new contracts. Crosville would sustain heavy financial losses as a result.

Whilst there was an urgent need to scale up operations to meet contractual obligations, there was also an urgent need to reduce costs if Love Lane depot was to survive. There was further pressure on the company as it also had to make sure that it remained viable for sale ahead of privatisation. These pressures would place a significant strain on both Crosville management and staff going forward as both attempted to deal with subsequent issues at the depot.

By this time Crosville's Love Lane depot had one resident driver instructor in the form of Bill Barlow, a seasoned Crosville professional. The training of 100 drivers could not be achieved by one instructor alone, as Bill Barlow recalls:

> Liverpool depot was supported by driver training instructors from Macclesfield (two) Runcorn (one) and Warrington (three) depots. They came over daily bringing their training buses with them. Our own training buses were G2 (612 LFM) and G166 (CFM 901C). At the time I was the only driving instructor at Liverpool as my colleague Les Stanton had recently transferred to South Wales Transport at Swansea depot. I was largely office based administrating the training programme during this period. The two training buses were used by the visiting instructors.

Sourcing twenty-three additional vehicles for the new contacts was proving difficult for the company as the UK second-hand bus market (outside Greater London) was also dealing with the effects of deregulation and increased need for additional vehicles as a result of new on-road competition.

Crosville initially drafted in buses from its Heswall and Macclesfield depots to meet the new commitments. Whilst driven initially by Liverpool drivers, they fell short of the long-standing agreement between the trade union and Crosville over the lack of MPTE-style cab doors, citing driver and farebox safety. The refusal to drive these vehicles resulted in lost mileage on the services in question.

The company then hired in thirty-six Daimler Fleetlines from MPTE. These vehicles were fitted with the MPTE cab doors but were slow in stark contrast to Crosville's lively DVLs, which had underpinned the long-standing timing test agreement between the trade union and Crosville. Unlike the five-gear semi-automatic Leyland-powered DVLs, the hired vehicles only had four gears and were Gardner powered.

Above: Bill Barlow in front of DFG166 at Edge Lane depot in the early 1980s. (Bill Barlow)

Below: Three driver training vehicles at Liverpool Love Lane depot following bus tender wins at deregulation. (Geoff O'Brien)

As Robert Montgomery comments: 'One of the notorious former MPTE Fleetlines acquired by Crosville's Love Lane depot after deregulation when the Liverpool operation was overwhelmed by new awards for tendered routes. 3006, now HDG936, in the depot yard, December 1986.' (Robert J. Montgomery)

The trade union branch agreed that the vehicles be driven initially by foregoing the timing test agreement in order to bring much-needed jobs to the depot. However, it quickly became clear that drivers found it impossible to keep to time, often running late on services and not finishing their working day on time. Complaints were subsequently made to the trade union branch to raise with company management.

Retiming the services to match slower vehicles but maintaining contractual service frequencies would have been a major problem for the company. Some routes were running at fifteen-minute intervals, which meant that additional drivers and vehicles would have been needed to maintain this if additional running time was added. The company was already struggling with costs, not to mention meeting the baseline resource requirement to operate the new contracts. Retiming the services would only exacerbate these issues further.

Due to operational difficulties other less suitable vehicles crept onto routes, such as single-deck Leyland Nationals powered by Gardner engines (SNGs), compounding concerns and frustrations even further. The trade union branch cited that this was putting drivers under immense pressure and creating unnecessary stress to a point that it believed that the company was putting profit before safety, commenting that concerns were falling on deaf ears. However, the company was eager to avoid increasing the losses it was already sustaining from operating these contracts.

Destination equipment on buses also became problematic, falling short of yet another long-standing agreement between the trade union branch and company. The MPTE Fleetlines were also well and truly past their best and suffered greatly from mechanical and reliability issues, with frequent breakdowns and fines imposed on Crosville by the MPTE for the non-operation of contracted services.

Significant pressures were now mounting on Crosville management as it was frantically trying to maintain services and contracts won whilst at the same time being confronted by increasing workforce unrest and rising costs. There was equal pressure on the trade union branch as it attempted to demonstrate to its membership that it was effectively engaging with company management, even though long-standing agreements were frustratingly being modified.

Due to the unreliability of the MPTE Daimler Fleetlines and the company's difficulty in finding vehicles with a level of equipment similar to its own, it ended up hiring ten Bristol VR double-deckers from Martins of Middlewich, which was a second-hand bus and coach dealer at the time.

Three of the 'hired in' PTE Daimler Fleetlines at Crosville Love Lane having been recovered following breakdowns, evident from the lower front section removed on each for towing. Destination blinds were also nonexistent. (Geoff O'Brien)

70

These vehicles had previously operated for West Midlands PTE (WMPTE) since the mid-1970s, before being withdrawn and sold to Martins. On the day the vehicles were driven from Martins to Crosville's Rock Ferry depot for preparation to enter service, only nine of the ten vehicles actually arrived, as one broke down on the way. Once prepared, they retained their blue and cream WMPTE livery with Crosville's new leaping lynx and fleet name overlayed, entering the fleet as HVG960 to HVG969.

Similar to the MPTE Daimler Fleetlines, the vehicles were slow in contrast to Crosville's DVLs and again only had four gears, and were powered by Gardner engines. Further to this they did not have power-assisted steering (PAS) and no such vehicles had been driven in Liverpool before on full 'OMO' duties, another long-standing agreement at Liverpool depot between the trade union branch and company.

The first time Liverpool drivers drove the hired vehicles from Martins, eight from eight reported them to the company and trade union for heavy steering. It wasn't the case that drivers were refusing to drive them, but more of signing them off with a fault.

By 31 December 1986 the trade union branch had researched other Crosville depots (English only by then) that had used double-deckers without PAS. All but one had used such vehicles in the past but only Chester, Ellesmere Port and Runcorn had used them in service, with a tendency to restrict use to school services, morning and afternoon.

One of the ex-Martins (WMPTE Bristol VRs) parked at Crosville's Rock Ferry depot being prepared for service, fleet number HVG960 (GOG 849N). (Geoff Smith)

The trade union branch had suggested to the company management that eight of the ten vehicles be redistributed across all company depots, one or two per depot. As part of this proposal the branch chairman and secretary also suggested that the remaining two at Liverpool depot be driven each day by them on their fixed part-day duties. Fixed duties for trade union officials were commonplace as it allowed them to work for Crosville, as well as undertake trade union business. The proposal of redistribution of the vehicles was refused by Crosville management.

In turn the trade union branch requested that they be withdrawn temporarily by the company so that any difficulties could be discussed through their long-established Joints Dispute Procedure. This was again refused by the company with the vehicles being allocated to regular service, citing that they were fit and would be driven, or drivers would be signed off pay.

On Monday 5 January 1987 drivers refused to drive them and were subsequently signed off pay, which led to strike action. A meeting took place between Crosville management and the trade union branch on Monday 12 January 1987 in which the company agreed to withdraw the ten vehicles pending a further meeting, with drivers returning to work on Tuesday 13 January.

Loaned from Martins (ex-WMPTE) and now Crosville HVG965, operating a staff-only service. (Geoff O'Brien)

On Wednesday 14 January, through agreement with Crosville management, all of the trade union branch committee members drove four of the vehicles to obtain an opinion on their steering. Whilst the committee thought that their steering was heavy, they agreed to put this forward to members in a branch meeting arranged for Friday 16 January. The branch requested a temporary solution with the company to allocate the vehicles on split duties from the first bus out on Monday 19 January. However, due to continuing vehicle shortage at Love Lane depot and pressures from the PTE and the Traffic Commissioner for lost mileage, this was refused by the company, with the vehicles being again allocated to the first buses out on Thursday 15 January. This was the day before the trade union branch meeting was to take place. It is believed that when drivers refused to drive the vehicles on the Thursday, they were told by the company to vacate the premises, resulting in immediate strike action.

A special negotiating committee met on Friday 23 January in Salford between the company and regional trade union representatives. This included a number of trade union branches from other Crosville depots, as well as Liverpool. The Regional Passenger Trade Group Secretary (RPTGS) stated that every effort should be made 'to achieve a settlement to the dispute at Liverpool', referring to the meeting that took place on 12 January. He aired his concern that sufficient time had not been allowed following this meeting for branch procedures to be followed to confirm the agreement representatives had made, which would have been recommended to the branch for acceptance. He said that because management had expectations that the buses would have been used in service it was the trade union's view that there was a 'lock-out' which started one day before a branch meeting had been called. His further view was that the situation had now hardened and that the only solution was to remove the ten ex-WMPTE (Martins) vehicles from Liverpool depot, with the remaining buses used to operate as many services as possible.

The RPTGS stated that other depots felt it appropriate to support Liverpool's actions but before this happened it was hoped that an agreement could be reached.

In the meeting, Crosville management confirmed the success of contract wins, and that after some delay the MPTE had made double-deckers available to cover the additional services. Their delay was caused by local trade union representatives at the MPTE, but some of the vehicles had failed to stand up to the work required of them. Management continued that a considerable amount of money had been spent trying to keep the MPTE vehicles on the road with serious under-operated mileage on both contract and commercial services.

Management confirmed that two matters had caused the company to seek the loan of the vehicles over a short-term period. The first was the result of the company undertaking an in-depth examination of service results and it being clear that the revenue projections provided by the MPTE were overly optimistic. Therefore, the company had notified the MPTE of its wish to terminate some of the contracts, with the termination notice date expiring on 7 March 1987, with vehicles needed to operate the services until then.

The second matter was a letter from the Traffic Commissioner seeking a response before 31 January 1987 as to why the company was not meeting its service obligations in the Liverpool area, with a number of sanctions being considered against Crosville. These would be available to the Traffic Commissioner after a public enquiry, which included the loss of three months' fuel duty grant for the whole company and the right to operate local bus services in a particular area, or indeed at all. These were all very grave and serious sanctions if imposed on Crosville.

Management commented that in an effort to improve the situation ten ex-WMPTE vehicles had been obtained on a short-term loan, and whilst these vehicles were not fitted with PAS they had been certified as roadworthy, six of them as recent as December 1986.

There was a meeting held on 23 December 1986 to discuss the proposed Boxing Day strike over pay rates not asked for at other depots. Management stated that trade union representatives had volunteered to give the vehicles a fair try but this was not the case when the vehicles were put forward.

Crosville confirmed that they did not want to put out any service that would be less than what was registered and that the ex-WMPTE vehicles would go a long way towards helping in this regard. The dispute was taking place against a background of considerable losses and drastic action was needed. Management acknowledged the problems that followed deregulation day, alleging that commercial mileage had been dropped in favour of maintaining contracted services, but the vehicles at the depot were inadequate for the amount of work. It was said that platform staff had made considerable effort to help, but the company was not in a position to be able to confirm whether the revenue projections made by the MPTE were accurate or not as full services had never been operated. Management continued that mileage was being lost on all types of services at Liverpool depot, with the main complaint being about service 107, which was being operated under contract to the MPTE.

Management confirmed that a number of vehicles would become surplus the following week from new minibus schemes introduced at other depots, although this wouldn't solve the problems presently being experienced at Liverpool. At the meeting it was said that Runcorn and Warrington depots could have helped but were not asked. Crosville claimed that the depots had been asked, but Runcorn depot was not prepared to cover the occasional journey and wanted the whole service or nothing.

The RPTGS accepted that a compromise had been reached on 12 January, but commented that management had not allowed sufficient time to go through union branch machinery. There was a wish to settle the difficulties as there was concern that this could spread to other depots.

The company agreed to feed spare vehicles from other depots as quickly as possible but on the understanding that they would be operated with existing cab doors until they could be modified. The vehicles were likely to be single deck and had to be cleared first with MPTE around contractual obligations for double-deckers to be waived. However, where necessary, to meet full-service obligations the ex-WMPTE vehicles would have to be driven to end of duty on 7 March 1987, with the vehicles being withdrawn beyond that date.

The RPTGS commented that the problem centred on Liverpool depot staff not being prepared to drive the ex-WMPTE vehicles and that services had to be covered by the company's own resources. To overcome the problem of cab doors, these should be removed from those fitted to the ex-WMPTE vehicles and fitted onto Crosville vehicles.

Crosville management stated that if accepted there would be a shortfall of service on the day staff resumed work and possibly for some time afterwards and as such they were not prepared to accept this position.

The trade union maintained its position in relation to the ex-WMPTE vehicles on the basis that they didn't have PAS. The trade union was concerned about their standard and unsuitability on the streets of Liverpool, and in their argument referred to a road test and operational trial of the Bristol VRT3 Eastern Coach Works double-decker with Hants & Dorset Motor Services in 1975. This was written by Martin Watkins in *Commercial Motor* on 5 December 1975, commenting that the vehicles tested had the optional manual steering fitted in place of power steering included in the Bristol standard specification. He continued that this made driving the fully loaded bus very hard work on the tight corners of Leicester's new test route and also made for a poor balance of energy the driver needed to expand on the different controls.

Crosville's counter argument was the fact that the same vehicles had been operated shortly before hire to the company on the streets of Birmingham since the 1970s without issue. The company stated that the cost to retrofit each vehicle with PAS was £1,000 and this was not economically viable for the company as they were only on hire.

The trade union branch had undertaken research into other similar NBC companies across the UK that had similar vehicles without PAS and learnt that they had either been retrofitted with power assist or had in fact been withdrawn and sold.

The research found that Alder Valley had Bristol VRs fitted and also carried out conversions for other companies; Bristol Omnibus Company had mass conversions done of Bristol VRs around 1982; Eastern National had converted twenty-six Bristol VRs in 1985; City of Oxford converted their Daimler Fleetlines in 1985; Lancaster City Transport were having PAS fitted to L registration Leyland Atlanteans; MPTE had sold ten single-deckers of N registration to Tyne and Wear PTE to be used at South Shields depot which were being equipped; Ribble had acquired G registration second-hand double-deckers which had been fitted; and West Yorkshire Road Car Co. had nineteen Bristol VRs fitted, the oldest being J registered.

Whilst Crosville had surrendered some of the contracts won, terminating on 7 March 1987, company management told the trade union that this was unlikely to cause staff redundancies at Liverpool depot as it was still short of drivers and had simply stopped recruiting. Crosville had to honour the operation of these contracts as a part of their contractual conditions until then.

The trade union was convinced that the company was trying to put a 'weak link in the chain' in an attempt to amend long-standing agreements and working conditions going forward. They were concerned about the increasing pressures being placed on a 'one person driver', driving older second-hand buses, collecting money, refuelling buses, parking buses, less running time and higher, more complicated fares. This went against a number of long-standing locally negotiated agreements between the trade union and Crosville management at Liverpool. The company was concerned that it was facing the possibility of a strike at Love Lane until 7 March and because of this the future of the company was truly at risk. NBC was equally concerned about the possibility that the company would be unsellable in terms of meeting its obligations regarding privatisation.

Subsequently, the drivers were all dismissed by the company through a letter dated 24 January 1987, which was issued two days later. The company deemed the hired-in vehicles from Martins to be roadworthy and refusing to drive roadworthy vehicles could have resulted in further issues at other depots. Crosville was also summoned before the Traffic Commissioner for failing to operate registered bus services.

Robert Montgomery comments: 'Love Lane depot, towards the end of the controversial dispute which resulted in the closure of the site soon after this date, 31 January 1987.' Note the destination blind on the double-decker (DVG497) on the left, 'S0D CHESTER', made up from numbers and destination. Chester was the company's head office at the time. It is clear that the relationship between the trade union branch and company management had sadly collapsed by this point. (Robert J. Montgomery)

It appears that the newly established disputes process put in place by the then government had not been followed correctly by the trade union as a secret ballot had not been called before striking. The trade union branch had sought union hierarchy support and advice with meetings taking place in London, but this was not forthcoming. The trade union branch cited that incorrect guidance had been provided to them.

In the 1980s the government of the time introduced a series of laws that restricted the rights of trade unions, limiting their right to strike, bringing back the 'sympathy strike' ban in 1980. This would be the first of seven Acts of Parliament that restricted trade union action, with the introduction of the Trade Union Act 1984 which required all trade unions to hold a secret ballot before calling a strike.

Some have commented that when the Tipp-Ex under the final issue date of the dismissal letter was scratched away it revealed two previous dates which matched strike dates. It appears that Crosville was waiting for NBC legal guidance and approval before issuing.

When all of the drivers were dismissed by the company a ten-day sit-in was staged by approximately fifty dismissed drivers at Love Lane depot, taking over the site and locking out management.

The High Sheriff of Lancashire and police arrive at Love Lane depot to serve an eviction notice to former Crosville staff on 4 February 1987. (Geoff O'Brien)

Eight days into the sit-in, an eviction notice was served by the High Sheriff of Lancashire, supported by the police, to the former staff on site. The sit-in came to an end two days later with former staff marched off the premises and the depot returned to company control.

Whilst the company was justifiably concerned during the period of sit-in, it is understood that no property was vandalised in any way. The vehicles used for the Mersey Link disabled transport service were also released without issue in recognition of the service they provided.

Days later, following the sit-in, former staff were invited back to Love Lane to hand back their company uniforms and claim outstanding holiday pay. A number have commented that there was an eery silence when they returned with only four of them allowed to enter the premises at a time with a police presence before leaving in the same way.

Crosville wrote a further letter to all dismissed staff on 28 January 1987 summarising the situation and explaining the company's actions. Some of the dismissed staff found alternative work with Liverbus, Merseybus, MTL and Timeline but many commented that that it was 'never the same as Crosville'.

A sombre and powerful image of crushed former Crosville staff vacating the Love Lane site following the sit-in. (Geoff O'Brien)

The Crosville men make their last stand at the Love Lane depot just before the bailiffs moved in to move them out

Playing the waiting game – busmen await their fate

Tears as busmen give up their sit-in

SACKED Liverpool bus drivers gave up their depot occupation yesterday just as bailiffs arrived to evict them.

Some put on brave smiles while others could scarcely hide the tears as they walked into the street, banners held high.

The 230 Crosville drivers had been staging a sit-in in protest at management's decision to close the depot.

They were sacked after going on strike in a dispute over the use of buses without power-assisted steering.

The drivers, who had fridges stocked up with food inside the Love Lane building, were thinking about staying put.

But they decided to give up peacefully when the High Court sheriff arrived.

"These lads are marching out to join the dole queue," said TGWU spokesman Ken Peeney. "It is a sad day."

Crosville says the Love Lane depot will not reopen.

Liverpool services will in future be served from depots outside the city.

Further talks are expected in London tomorrow between union and management.

Meanwhile, no Crosville services are running in Liverpool, but buses in Wirral are running normally.

Meanwhile, trade unionists in Wirral have launched a campaign for buses to be equipped with assault screens, after a Wallasey driver was attacked and robbed by a gang of youths.

Robert Meadows was beaten up after the gang refused to pay the 60p Merseybus fare on the the No 10 route from Clatterbridge to New Brighton.

After the attack, which left the driver shocked and with facial injuries, the gang made off with his cash box.

A press clipping from the *Liverpool Daily Post* on 5 February 1987. (Liverpool Daily Post/Reachplc)

7

The Silent Depot

Les A. Smith was a garage foreman at Love Lane depot, having started work with Crosville in 1969. His father before him, Mr A. B. Smith, had also been a garage foreman with Crosville in Liverpool, starting work with the company in the 1940s after the end of the Second World War and putting in an impressive thirty-five years of service with Crosville.

A large number of vehicles are seen tightly parked in a now-lifeless Love Lane depot. (Les A. Smith)

Les, or baby A. B. as he was affectionately called by his Crosville friends, stayed on at Love Lane depot after its closure, charged with looking after the premises. The following images were taken at that time and are certainly poignant. They represent an eery period post-closure in which the depot stood empty, sombre, and silent, devoid of any life and movement, with its spirt now crushed. The end of Crosville in Liverpool.

A row of double-deckers parked next to each other in a silent Love Lane yard. (Les A. Smith)

Some of the ex-WMPTE Bristol VRs at Love Lane. The auxiliary breakdown vehicle is seen on the right, no longer required. (Les A. Smith)

One of the loaned ex-WMPTE Bristol VRs parked in front of the depot's offices. (Les A. Smith)

8

Personal Recollection of Paul Rycroft

Paul Rycroft worked for Crosville in the 1970s and 1980s at both Liverpool Edge Lane and Love Lane depots. Paul has provided his personal recollections of his time at Love Lane as matters at the depot worsened. In his spare time away from Crosville, Paul was also a Naval Reservist.

Paul Rycroft in the Naval Reserves. (Paul Rycroft)

Here are my recollections of the build-up to the demise of Crosville Liverpool at Love Lane depot. I must add that these are my personal memories of that time.

I worked for Crosville from 1972 until its closure. It was in my mind a really good job. It was a close-knit workforce, and everyone knew everyone else; many of the staff had worked for the company for many years even though the pay and conditions were better if we had worked for the MPTE. It has been said that during the approach of the closure that threats of violence were made to staff who didn't want to take on the fight. I never saw or heard of any of this going on.

It's been stated that Liverpool depot was very militant and were a pain in the side of the management, which I suppose we were. But the people of Liverpool have always stood up for their rights and never kowtowed to the whips of the management.

I was not and have never been what you would call militant but I do stand up for what I feel is right and yes, some of the strikes were a pain, especially as I had a young family then and received nothing for striking.

The other depots always criticised us for the strikes but still accepted the many benefits we fought for: shift allowance, overtime pay and many more. They took them but left us to fight for them and complained about us.

In 1986, deregulation came about. Everyone knew it was a very bad idea but the government went ahead anyway. The first day was ridiculous with buses not knowing where they were going as no real route training had been given. These were all new routes in parts of the city we had never ventured to before and had always classed as being out of our area.

Because of the increase of routes, we did not have enough vehicles. So the management bought some old buses from somewhere. I don't know where and there were lots of rumours about them coming from a scrap yard but I don't know if it was true. They certainly wouldn't be out of place in a scrap yard is what I do know.

These vehicles had power steering but it didn't work. Now if anyone has ever tried to drive a power-assisted car without the power assistance working they will know it's very hard. Well multiply that by 10 for a bus. Some have said its OK if you don't try and make sharp turns too slow. These have obviously never driven a bus through a crowded Liverpool city centre and then into the countryside.

The drivers were literally having to stand up in the cab to get the purchase to turn the wheel. This brought about many comments from the public who were watching this.

Well obviously the drivers started signing the buses off as defective because of the power steering. They went into the engineers shed and came out again as unrepairable.

We did find out later that the fitters had been told to do nothing and just say alterations had been done, but they refused to lie like that.

When one driver refused to take one of these vehicles out after just moving it from one side of the large yard to the other he was immediately suspended.

This caused an immediate walk-out by the drivers as they thought quite rightly this was a safety issue.

Love Lane depot. A mix of Crosville, hired MPTE and ex-WMPTE vehicles are seen here. (Geoff O'Brien)

After a meeting the following day everyone agreed to return as they had been told this wouldn't happen again. After another day it did happen again and the same thing happened. This went on into January '87 with them trying to force these vehicles onto the road. We then voted to remain on strike until these buses were removed.

At that time the Thatcher government had been changing the law regarding strikes and it was quite complicated. We asked the TGWU if this strike was lawful and their paid official stood up in front of 300 men and said it was.

We then all received a letter dated 24 January 1987 stating as we were taking part in an illegal strike and we were dismissed with immediate effect.

The date on the letter had the number 20 written in ballpoint under the Tipp-Ex. I scraped away the Tipp-Ex to find several dates written underneath which were the dates we had walked out; I think there was at least three other dates.

This to me proved that the company had full intention to use these strikes to close the depot without having to pay any redundancy money out, but on the previous dates we had gone back to work so they were unable to issue them.

We heard the same twaddle from the other depots and of course they didn't learn as they had done the same thing to other depots, resulting in Crosville England disappearing, leaving only Crosville Wales, which of course also went eventually.

83

Paul recalls the final day at Love Lane depot, which involved returning uniforms. The following account is very powerful and full of emotion and demonstrates clearly the impact the situation had on real people.

> The part about the day we had to return our uniform was a very sober day. I had forgotten about the police being there in case we took over the depot again, but the fight had been well knocked out of us.
>
> When we went into the depot, they had a table across the door as a makeshift counter. There was a sign saying ALL items of uniform must be returned.
>
> The person taking the uniform off us was a depot inspector called Frank Robinson. He was one of the nicest men you could ever wish to meet. His normal job was to maintain the Setright ticket machines and he was also the first person any new employee met as he took everyone through their employment paperwork and did all the ticket machine training. I never saw or heard of anyone ever having a bad word with or about him. I remember on that day he was so visibly upset at what was happening and found it difficult to look at anyone directly as I'm sure he would have broken down. As for all items of uniform, he just took the bags from everyone and tossed them into a pile in the canteen; he wasn't going to count it all. It was sad that day as for most it would be the last day we saw each other, until the unfair dismissal hearing, which favoured the employer.

George Taylor, on the left, and Frank Robinson on 18 January 1985. (Bill Barlow)

I also remember when having to sign off for unemployment benefit, at that time if you were sacked you had to wait a certain number of weeks before benefit was paid (say four weeks) and if you resigned it was double the number of weeks. But even the DHSS decided in our favour and we received benefit straight away.

Paul comments that Mr Robinson outside the world of Crosville was also a founder member of the Merseysippi Jazz Band. Paul continued that he thinks that it was Mr Robinson himself that came up with the band's name when they formed after the Second World War. They played at the Cavern in Liverpool before the Beatles and also played with Louis Armstrong no less.

Mr Frank Robinson sadly passed away on 30 December 2010. Our thoughts are very much with his family.

Paul's account echoes the emotions and feelings of so many others, some of whom have only recently begun to speak about what happened out of fear of provoking the deep upset and grief that was felt at the time.

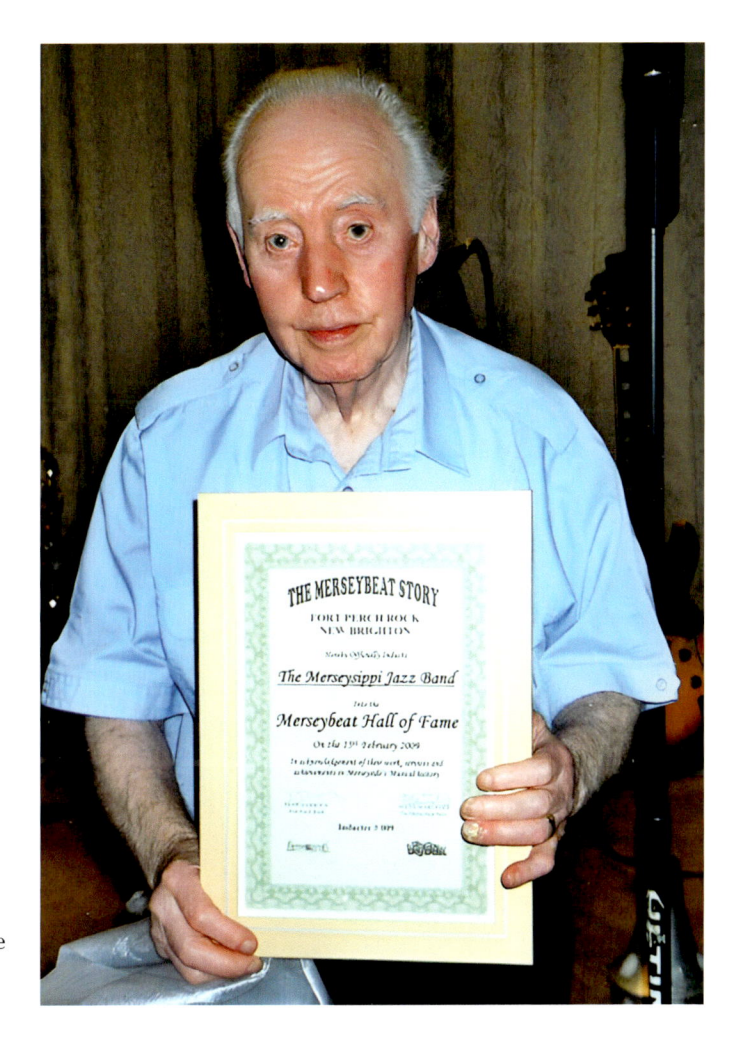

Frank Robinson with the Merseysippi Jazz Band's certificate of entry into the Merseybeat Hall of Fame. (Fred Burnett)

85

9

Mr Robert Parry MP

(HC Deb, 25 February 1987, vol. 111, c284)

In the 1970s Britain suffered economic difficulties and a steady rise in unemployment. The situation in Liverpool, though, went from bad to worse in the early 1980s, with endless factory closures and some of the highest unemployment rates in the country. In 1985 unemployment in Liverpool exceeded 20 per cent, around double the national average.

Mr Robert Parry was a Labour politician and Member of Parliament in Liverpool for twenty-seven years, having been elected to the Liverpool City Council for the Central ward in 1963. He was elected to Parliament at the 1970 election for Liverpool Exchange, Liverpool Scotland Exchange from 1974 and then Liverpool Riverside from 1983 to his retirement in 1997; he passed away on 9 March 2000.

On 16 January 1986 in the House of Commons Mr Robert Parry MP addressed the House on increasing poverty and urban deprivation and the problems in the inner-city areas of Liverpool. He commented on the need to regenerate Britain's cities and deliberate the reduction of rate support grant and investment in housing, which was leading to a major housing crisis and homelessness.

On 25 February 1987 in a Commons sitting Mr Robert Parry MP sought leave to move an Adjournment of the House, under Standing Order No. 20, for the purpose of discussing what he referenced as a specific and important matter that should have urgent consideration: namely, the closure of the Love Lane bus depot and the sacking of 270 transport workers by the Crosville bus company, Liverpool. He said that the matter was specific because it dealt with the sacking of 270 workers, many of them long-serving employees, and the closure of a bus depot in his constituency, which had the highest unemployment level on the British mainland.

He went on to state that the matter was important because more than 150 of the sacked workers had between ten and twenty-five years of service with the company and one had more than thirty years of service and was only two years from retirement age. He said that none of these workers had received or would receive a penny in redundancy pay and that it was an absolute disgrace.

He said that the matter should receive urgent consideration because the sacking followed a strike by the bus drivers who refused to drive old second-hand buses – some fourteen years old with no power steering. He stated that Crosville's action might encourage other bus companies to follow its scandalous lead, thus endangering the lives of not only bus drivers and passengers but pedestrians and road users. He hoped, for these reasons, that the Speaker of the House would grant his application.

Mr Robert Parry MP's application was not granted and cited as not appropriate under Standing Order No. 20.

10

Crosville Beyond Love Lane

Crosville was one of the last companies to be sold in the breakup of the National Bus Company. On the order of the Secretary of State, Crosville was to be sold as separate Wales and England companies, the former ending in a management buyout, thereby creating a new company with 470 vehicles. Meanwhile, operations in England remained

DOG126 in Crosville's second post-deregulation livery on Brownlow Hill, Liverpool, on 19 July 1989. (Robert J. Montgomery)

as Crosville Motor Services Ltd, which went to new owners on 25 March 1988 with 1,169 staff and, coincidentally, also 470 vehicles. The purchaser was ATL Holdings based in South Yorkshire. They had already bought National Travel East Ltd, as well as Yelloway of Rochdale. However, ATL had run into difficulties due to their inexperience in running bus companies, in particular around maintenance. Yelloway were stripped of various local authority contracts, Crosville then taking over its remaining bus operations from their Rochdale depot.

Less than a year later Crosville (the England half) was sold by ATL, this time to the Drawlane group on 18 February 1989. It was announced that Crosville would return to its former flagship status, but sadly this never happened. Heswall depot was closed on 4 September 1988 with its vehicle fleet reallocated to Rock Ferry depot. Drawlane already owned near neighbours North Western and Midland Red North and as such saw an opportunity from 11 September 1989 to rationalise operations between its subsidiaries. This involved routes across Liverpool being interlinked when Skelhorne Street bus station closed.

Crosville's headquarters at Crane Wharf was closed during the second week of May 1989, moving close by to Walls Avenue, a street that once housed Crosville engineering units, last used in the early 1950s.

DOG156 in its PMT-Crosville livery, now renumbered DOG785, approaching Woodside, Birkenhead, mid-morning on 30 June 1994. (Robert J. Montgomery)

Former Crosville SNL657, now North Western 347, travelling along Brownlow Hill, Liverpool, on 18 July 1994. (Robert J. Montgomery)

In autumn 1989, Drawlane carried out major depot transfers to neighbouring subsidiaries. On 27 November Crosville's Runcorn and Warrington operations were transferred to North Western; Crewe depot went to Midland Red North; and Congleton, Macclesfield, Rochdale and Bredbury were taken over by the Beeline Buzz Company. At the end of the following January Northwich also went to Midland Red North.

Just one week later, on 2 February 1990, Crosville's remaining depots at Chester (The Rink), Ellesmere Port, West Kirby and Rock Ferry were sold to PMT Ltd of Stoke-on-Trent, who also purchased the rights to the Crosville name. As a result, Crosville Motor Services Ltd was renamed North British Bus Limited from 30 March 1990 but by then its bus operations had ceased. The head office in Walls Avenue closed four months later.

PMT was sold to Badgerline in June 1995, which in turn merged with the GRT Group, forming First Bus. The Crosville name in England was slowly ebbing away into history.

A subsequent management buyout of Drawlane's bus operations created British Bus, which in turn was bought in 1996 by the Cowie Group of Sunderland. A year later the company was renamed Arriva with a corporate livery of aquamarine and stone, rolled out in 1998. The British Bus/Arriva portfolio had grown with a number of UK acquisitions, including Crosville Wales from National Express and later all the bus operations of the troubled MTL Ltd, based in Liverpool. On 2 April 1998 Crosville Wales Ltd was renamed

Arriva Cymru Ltd and thus the Crosville name was consigned to history. By a quirk of acquisitions, Arriva, with its common livery, was now serving territory akin to the original Crosville area, though eroded within by First Group, Stagecoach and various independents, large and small. Meanwhile, the name of Crosville lives on only in the form of preserved vehicles, various social media groups and publications.

The old Crosville depots at Edge Lane and Love Lane may have gone but the memories from both locations remain. The former Edge Lane depot site is now a car park. Pensarn Road, the row of houses that backs up against the former site, as captured in so many photos of the time, is the only visible remaining landmark.

The Love Lane site became a bus depot once again when it was occupied by the North Western Road Car Company in 1989, with some of the former Crosville drivers and vehicles returning, ironically, but now working for a different company. The site is now a housing estate, completely oblivious of what occurred there nearly forty years ago.

Former DOG171 in First PMT livery, now as DOG891 at Northgate Street, Chester, on 8 August 1998. The Crosville fleet name has now been relegated to a small token gesture under the driver's cab window in favour of the First branding. (Robert J. Montgomery)

91

Above: During North Western's tenure, Love Lane depot workshops on the left and offices on the right. (Brian Moore collection)

Below: Love Lane depot's engineering facilities. (Brian Moore collection)

Conclusion

There has been much speculation over the years about the cause of the sad closure of Crosville's Love Lane depot in Liverpool, with opinions divided. Some have blamed company management whilst others have blamed the trade union.

In reality all involved were victims of circumstances brought on by the effects of deregulation and the impact of major (well intentioned by management) contract wins.

Company management was under significant pressure on a number of fronts, which only intensified throughout 1986 and into 1987 as it frantically attempted to meet imposed requirements in the lead-up to deregulation and the challenges thereafter.

Significant increasing pressures were subsequently placed on staff, most notably drivers and engineers, intensifying in the same way. The trade union's duty was to represent and protect its members to the best of its ability and this in the face of constantly increasing challenges resulted in long-standing agreements being modified to the detriment of staff.

There were major pressures on all sides as UK legislation changed the way buses would be run across the UK outside Greater London and the mammoth tasks that were subsequently involved with the transition.

David A. Jones, Crosville's Mersey Valley District manager at the time, comments:

> If I had to sum the whole sad debacle up in a few words, I would say that the rushed introduction of the provisions of the 1985 Act gave both the company management, the trade union's officers and the rank and file employees too little time to adjust to a political and economic landscape which was the complete antithesis of every certainty they had known and understood throughout their working lives. The same pressures were evident everywhere in the bus industry, but were perhaps more intense in Liverpool due to the greater historical tensions between employers and labour in that city.

The closure of Love Lane depot had a profound impact on Crosville and its staff. The winning of new contracts should have been extremely positive in the face of deregulation.

In reality due to the numbers won, associated low prices and high cost it only acted as a catalyst that eroded the relationship between the trade union and company management to a point of no return, as trust, respect and engagement broke down completely.

The period spanning 1986 and into 1987 was a perfect storm for the company and staff. Recognising and accepting that deregulation would change everything forever was difficult or even impossible as it brought profound and significant challenges and changes for both company and staff and was outside their control.

The hard-hitting fact is that 270 people lost their jobs with the sudden closure of Love Lane depot. Crosville had a proud heritage in Liverpool spanning sixty-five years, made so by very proud people. Suddenly it was all gone.

The situation remains raw to many today, nearly forty years later. The words significant and profound have been carefully chosen to convey the impact of what happened to real people and their families. Hopefully this book has provided greater detail and clarity, not previously known or published, having been collated from actual Crosville and trade union officials and documents of the time.

Robert J. Montgomery remembers how quickly the closure came after the ex-WMPTE vehicles from Martins were not driven due to safety concerns raised. Dismissal notices were issued to all on Friday 26 January and by Monday 23 February, Robert began new employment with MTL at its Edge Lane garage, like so many of his colleagues and friends. Beyond Crosville, Bill Barlow went on to work for MTL at Birkenhead and spent the following thirty years at its Laird Street depot. This would be in addition to the fifteen years he'd already served at Crosville – a bus industry career spanning an impressive forty-five years.

Graham Warren, the son of the late George Warren, one of the 'legends' of Crosville's Edge Lane and Love Lane depots, poignantly recalls:

> I remember the state my Dad was in, that his 'beloved' Crosville was gone.
>
> He spent one and a half days at Shearings, operating his old Crosville routes, till he just quit on the second day, as he was too distraught and overcome with emotion.
>
> A few weeks later, he got a start at Merseybus, Gillmoss garage, where he stayed for nearly four years, it was a bitter pill to swallow for him now working for what was once 'the old PTE', but he was never the same once Crosville had finished.
>
> He then went to work for Liverbus in 1991, where he was happier, until he was forced to medically retire at the start of 1992.
>
> Such a sad end to his once happy career.

Graham added: 'I will defend my Dad's honour to the hilt, he was never a militant. His blood was green with a white band (Crosville colours), but being Scouse, he'd never cross a picket line. Ultimately, he paid the price, but kept his head held high.'

These are such powerful words full of emotion and rightly so. Sadly, Mr Warren passed away on 23 September 2016. Our thoughts are very much with Graham and his family as we remember Mr Warren, the legend of Edge Lane. We also remember other members of the Crosville family in the same way who are sadly no longer with us.

The late George Warren. (Graham Warren)

The late Mr George Warren's Crosville uniform, kept in pristine condition to this day. (Graham Warren)

95

Graham has retained his dad's Crosville uniform to this day, which hangs in pristine condition in his wardrobe in memory of his late father, with his driver's badge, number 83873, taking pride of place on his driving jacket.

What actually happened at Crosville's Love Lane depot is only known ultimately by those who were involved at the time.

The purpose of this book is not to reopen old wounds, but to tell the story of what actually happened and through the human lens, revealing the true impact and loss to real people and their families. To debate the rights or wrongs of deregulation is also not the intention, but its impact at Crosville in Liverpool is quite clear. This book has been produced following extensive research, carefully ensuring the utmost respect and sensitivity to all concerned at all times.

We remember the proud and professional staff who worked for Crosville in Liverpool, spanning its sixty-five-year existence in the city, and whose wish was simply to do an honest day's work and provide for their families.

In memory of Crosville Motor Services, Crosville Wales and all of its staff from all depots with utmost respect.

A more up-to-date photograph taken on Tuesday 20 August 2024 at the former location of Crosville's Edge Lane depot. Along with my youngest son and father, I had travelled to Liverpool to catch up with former Crosville staff, and their descendants, mentioned in the book and to have a group photograph taken. Some people hadn't seen each other in nearly forty years. From left to right: Richard Lloyd Jones (author), Gethin Lloyd-Jones (author's youngest son), Richard Lloyd Jones (author's late father), Malcolm Davies, Robert J. Montgomery, Graham Warren, David Forrest, Geoff O'Brien, Raymond Patterson, Mike Lambden, Bill Barlow, Allan Bentley, Bob Hayden, John Embleton, Paul Rycroft and Melvin Robinson.